Battleship TIRPITZ

Gerhard Koop
Klaus-Peter Schmolke

CONWAY
MARITIME PRESS

Jacket illustrations:
Front: *Tirpitz* in 1944.
A model of *Tirpitz* as she appeared in 1943-4.
Back: Internal profile and deck plan.

First published in Germany as 'Vom Originale zum modell: Schlatschiff *Tirpitz*

First published in Britain by
Conway Maritime Press,
a division of Batsford Communications PLC,
583 Fulham Road
LONDON SW6 5BY

This edition specially published for
The Military Book Club,
Doubleday Direct,
1540 Broadway,
New York, NY 10036

ISBN 0-85177-773-2

Translated by Lt Col Bernd E P Rolff
Designed by Simon Ray-Hills
Printed in Hong Kong

Contents

Tirpitz **underway in 1943, seen from one of the many harbour protection vessels.**

Preface

This publication covers the battleship *Tirpitz* with reference to *Bismarck*. It contains the most important technical information along with a brief history of battleship development. There are numerous detailed photographs of the ship and machinery used in both *Tirpitz* and *Bismarck*, some of which are rare, and there are also many photographs of a model of *Tirpitz* which was built for the Kuestenmuseum in Wilhelmshaven.

The drawings of *Tirpitz*, all in the uniform scale of 1:300, are smaller-scale renderings of those which accompanied the first German edition of the book. It is hoped that this collection of data, specifications, photographs and line drawings will provide the modeller and shiplover with all essential information on his chosen subject, and direct him to further sources of research material.

I especially wish to thank Mr Klaus-Peter Schmolke, who patiently spent many hours drawing plans and sketches, and also Dr Reinhardt, the custodian of the Kuestenmuseum, Wilhelmshaven, who kindly gave permission for photographs to be taken of the *Tirpitz* model. Last but not least I wish to extend my thanks to my friend Mr F Bavendamm, who, with his usual organisation and skill, took all the photographs of the model.

Gerhard Koop

The beginning and the end: *Tirpitz* prior to her launch, seen from a forward position on starboard. Note the size of the break shield with its console and also the anchor which is clear for the launch...

... *Tirpitz* as a wreck, a few weeks after she capsized. Salvage operations are still underway.

History of the development of battleships

Tirpitz was the last and also the largest and most modern battleship built for the German *Kriegsmarine*, the naval branch of the national-socialist German armed forces, the *Wehrmacht*. Because of the war, other larger and even more powerful units never reached completion. The ones that were already laid down were broken up again, and other developments never got any further than the drawing board.

In the beginning was the sailing ship. Until the nineteenth century, large sailing warships with three masts and high freeboard, carrying a large number of guns on the broadside, were the backbone of every seafaring nation and especially of the two naval superpowers Great Britain and France. There were no uniform classes, warships were simply classified by the number of guns. Battle tactics emphasised parallel lines of ships exchanging broadsides. It was these tactics which later led to the designation 'ship of the line', also referred to poetically as 'wooden walls'.

Following the invention of the steam engine and the paddle wheel and screw propeller, navies converted existing sailing ships and new ships were equipped with the new propulsion. The advantage of steam propulsion was obvious, as steam-powered ships could easily outmanoeuvre any sailing ship. Further developments followed in the mid-nineteenth century. The muzzle-loading gun was gradually replaced by the breechloader, new projectiles were developed, round shot gave way to shells, and rifled guns replaced the smoothbore. From then on shells could be fired with a higher muzzle velocity, which again led to guns with longer ranges.

In the 1850s, warships in Germany were also referred to as 'screw ships of the line'. They were still sailing ships but were equipped with steam engines, and were two-deckers and three-deckers with guns on the broadsides. Because of the rapid development of weapons technology, ships soon had to be armoured. At first, thick wood and other materials were tried, but Krupp in Germany and other manufacturers elsewhere soon developed suitable iron and steel armour.

In the second half of the century, the screw ship of the line evolved into the 1st class armoured ship. Originally these ships had a broadside armament (from approximately 1858 to 1865) but that gave way to the central battery ship. In parallel, the casemate ship was introduced by 1865 and was used until around 1875 before being upstaged by the turret ship which appeared in 1875 and was still being built approximately twenty years later.

By this time in Germany the capital ship was described as the *Linienschiff* 'ship of the line', a designation which had to give way to *Großlinienschiff* 'large ship of the line' after *Dreadnought* had appeared in 1905. The final step was the *Schlachtschiff* 'battleship', the last examples of which are the *Iowa*-class of the US Navy.

In the German Navy, this development was slow. The first units of this type were mainly solitary and usually designed and built abroad, often in Great Britain and France. Other ships were acquired second-hand. There was no uniformity at all in respect of size, appearance, armament, machinery, or speed. In the German Navy (until 1867 the Prussian Navy, from 1867 - 1871 the North German Federal Navy, after 1871 the Imperial Navy), distinctions were made between armoured frigates and armoured corvettes, both of which came under the general designation armoured ships. According to an order dated 29 August 1893, armoured ships had to be divided into three different groups, I, II or III. Another order followed on the 27 February 1899 cancelling classes II and III, and re-designating the ships of class 1 under a new and uniform designation *Linienschiff*.

This designation was retained - even though the units of the *Nassau*-class were also referred to as large ships of the line - until the end of the 1930s. The German ships of this type always sported certain uniform features: heavy main armament with uniform calibre (there were a few exceptions), a strong secondary armament arranged in casemates, and more or less similar machinery and speed. This enabled the ships to fight in a line of battle, according to the then valid tactical regulations. The last battle of this kind was the Battle of Jutland, which took place on 31 May 1916.

New methods were applied when Germany built its first battleships in the early twentieth century: they became larger and faster. The armament was not changed very much, but the guns themselves were modernized with new control systems. The armour was made of improved material. But the days of these giants of the seas were numbered as a new weapon arrived on the scene: the aircraft. The Second World War clearly proved that even the largest and most powerful ships were unable to ignore this threat. In May 1941, *Bismarck* was brought to action by this new weapon and, seven months later, the British ships *Repulse* and *Prince of Wales* followed suit. The war in the Pacific sealed the fate of the capital ship. The large seapowers drew their conclusions, and from then on their battleships only took part in joint operations with carriers or air forces, one protecting the other. After the war most of these battleships were scrapped.

Operation Rösselsprung, July 1942. A view from *Tirpitz* with other heavy units astern. Directly behind *Tirpitz* is *Admiral Scheer*, and behind this cruiser is *Admiral Hipper*. In the foreground 38cm turret C is being painted by sailors.

***Tirpitz,* 31 March 1944. Note the elevated platform behind the mainmast which had to be fitted to carry the radar set Würzburg-Gerät.**

Technical data of Tirpitz

Displacement, official:	35,000 tons (35,560 tons)
Displacement, design (1941):	45,474 tons
Displacement (1941):	49,429 tons
Displacement, full load (1944):	53,500 tons
Length overall:	253.6m
Length waterline:	241.72m
Beam:	36m
Design draught 1935:	9.9m
Max. draught (at 53,890t):	10.61m
Side height:	15m
Shaft horsepower design:	138,000
maximum:	163,026
Speed, design:	29 knots
Speed, maximum:	30.8knots
Range:	8,870nm at 19 knots 9,280nm at 16 knots
Complement (1943):	108 officers 2,500 men
Machinery:	12 x Wagner high-pressure boilers superheated 3 x sets geared turbines 3 x shafts with one 4.8m propeller each 2 x rudders
Power supply:	2 x power plants with four diesel generators 500kW each, 2 x power plants with five turbo generators 690kW and one turbo generator 460kW, each 1 x power plant with one diesel generator 550kVA
Equipment:	4 x aircraft Aradao Ar 196 7 x searchlights 14 x boats 3 x bow anchors 1 x stern anchor
Armament:	8 x 38cm/L47 in four twin mountings 12 x 15cm/L55 in six twin mountings 16 x 10.5cm/L65 AA guns in eight twin mountings 16 x 3.7cm/L83 AA guns in twin mountings 12 x 2cm AA guns in twin and quadruple mountings, later 78 8 x 53.3cm torpedo tubes in two quadruple mountings
Fire control arrangements	5 x 10.5m base rangefinders 1 x 7m base rangefinder 2 x 6.5m base rangefinders 4 x AA director control towers
Radar:	radar sets FuMO mounted on the foretop, the fore conning tower and the aft conning tower

Armour protection (compared with Bismarck):

Most of the armour plating used for armour protection consisted of KC armour steel.
KC - Krupp cemented, i.e. carbon content 0.34%, nickel content 3.78%, manganese content 0.31%, and chrome content 2.06%. There were two classifications for armour steel: Ww - Wotan, weich (Wotan, soft); and Wh - Wotan, hart (Wotan, hard). Wh had a rupture resistance of 85-95kg/mm^2, a strain of 20% and a yield point of 50-55kg/mm^2. Ww had a rupture resistance of 65-70kg/mm^2, a strain of 25% and a yield point of 38-40kg/mm^2.

Belt:	300mm KC, tapering to 270mm at the top tapering to 170mm at the bottom
Citadel:	145mm KC on 50mm teak backing
Hull front:	60mm Wh, welded
rear:	80mm Wh, welded
Bulkhead upper part of the hull:	25mm Wh, welded

Bulkhead below armour deck between torpedo bulkheads:	200mm Wh
Transverse armour bulkhead to upper platform deck from outer plating to torpedo bulkhead:	100mm Wh
Transverse armour bulkhead under the upper platform deck between torpedo bulkheads:	80mm Wh
Transverse armour bulkhead under the upper platform deck between torpedo bulkhead and outer plating:	20mm Wh
Longitudinal torpedo bulkhead:	45mm Ww, riveted
Armour deck:	80mm Wh, riveted
Armour deck above magazines:	100mm Wh
Armour deck forecastle:	30mm Wh
Armour deck aft:	80mm Wh
Armour deck above steering gear:	100mm Wh
Upper deck:	50mm Wh, welded
Upper deck around turrets:	80mm Wh, welded
Barbettes of 38cm turrets:	340mm KC (front, middle) 340mm KC (sides) 340mm KC (rear) 220mm (rear, *Tirpitz*)
38cm turrets:	360mm KC (front) 220mm KC (sides) 320mm KC (rear) 180mm KC (roof, front) 180mm KC (roof, rear)
15cm turrets:	100mm KC (front) 40mm KC (sides) 40mm KC (rear) 40mm KC (roof)
10.5cm	shields 20mm
Fore conning tower:	350mm KC (sides, slope) 200mm KC (roof) 220mm KC (access tunnel) 70mm KC (deck)
Aft conning tower:	150mm KC (sides, slope) 50mm KC (access tunnel)
Upper armour belt:	145mm KC
Slope of armour belt, midships and at the ends:	320mm KC (*Bismarck*) 315MM KC (*Tirpitz*) (tapering to 170mm)

DECKS

Upper deck above machinery centre:	50mm Wh (*Bismarck* and *Tirpitz*)
Upper deck above magazines centre:	80mm Wh (*Bismarck* and *Tirpitz*)
Slope above machinery centre:	110mm Wh (*Bismarck* and *Tirpitz*)
Slope above magazines centre:	110mm Wh (*Bismarck* and *Tirpitz*)
Armour deck above machinery centre:	50mm Wh (*Tirpitz*) 80mm Wh (*Bismarck*)
Armour deck above magazines centre:	100mm Wh (*Tirpitz*) 95mm Wh (*Bismarck*)
Slope above machinery:	110mm Wh (*Bismarck* and *Tirpitz*)
Slope above magazines:	120mm Wh (*Bismarck* and *Tirpitz*)

SIDE PROTECTION:

Turret A down to 3.05m	bulkhead 53mm torpedo bulkhead 45mm
Turret B down to 3.51m	bulkhead 53mm torpedo bulkhead 45mm
Midship section down to 5.5m	bulkhead 53mm torpedo bulkhead 45mm
Turret C down to 3.35m	bulkhead 53mm torpedo bulkhead 45mm
Turret D down to 3.05m	bulkhead 53mm torpedo bulkhead 45mm
Rangefinder conning tower	100mm KC (horizontal) 200mm KC (slope)
Rangefinder aft conning tower	50mm KC (horizontal) 150mm KC (slope)
Foretop	20mm (horizontal) 60mm (sides)
Rangefinders	20mm (horizontal) 50mm (sides)

UNDERWATER PROTECTION:

The ship was protected from explosive charges up to 250kg TNT. The width of the armour protection was 5.5m, and the longitudinal bulkheads were 53mm thick. The whole protective system had a depth of 1.7m. The safety zone for the citadel provided immunity against hits from 38.1cm shells (15in) weighing 1,016kg between 10,973m and 21,031m (for the machinery) and to 23,319m (for the magazines).

Application and distribution of the armour protection

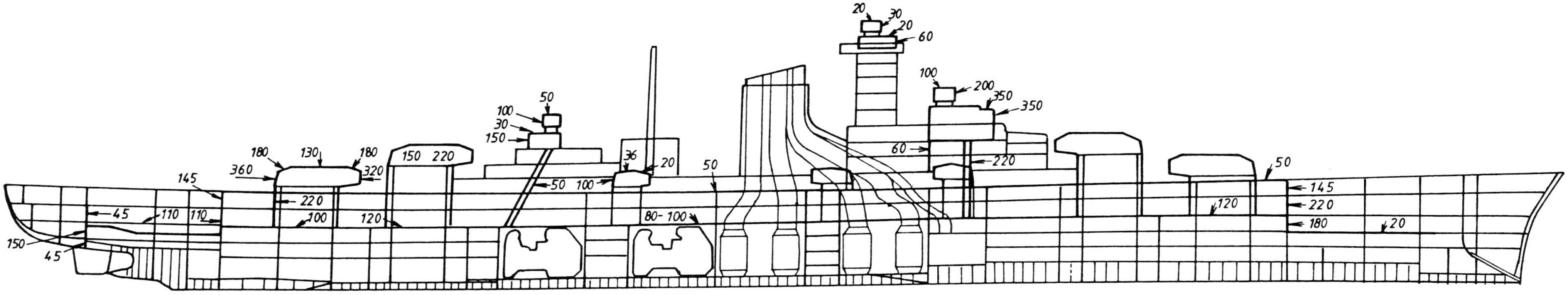

Inboard profile

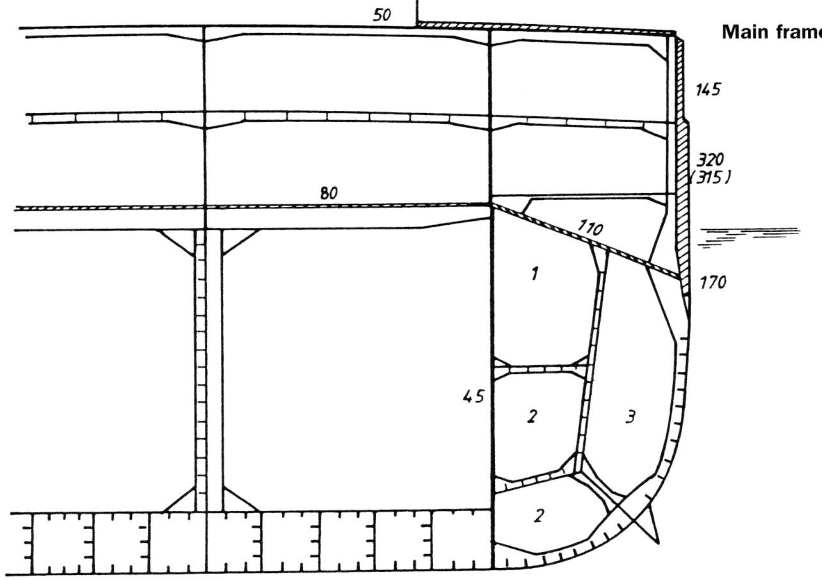

Main frame

1 - feedwater cell

2 - fuel oil tank

3 - terreplein

Operating instructions and manuals (general account)

By the time she is commissioned a ship has received her final outfit of equipment and supplies: fuel and lubricants, ammunition, tools, spare parts, and, of course, provisions. The ship's equipment also includes all plans, drawings and other documents directly relating to the ship, including: calculations on displacement; body plans; drawings decribing the results of calculations; sectional drawings of the structure; room distribution plans; dock drawings; design drawings; drawings of the rig; accomodation plans; plans on stability; calculations on leakage; calculations on pump capacities and flooding valves; drawings of the mainframe, the frames at bow and stern and of the turrets; drawings of stem and stern with the rudders; steering, shafts and shaft brackets; drawings of the plating of the hull, the load line and the ship's bottom; drawings of the arrangement of armour plates and armour protection; detailed drawings of anchors, boats and associated tackle; masts; ammunition lifts; valves of fresh water tanks; ventilation plant; conning towers; means of communication; compass plans; magazines and ammunition transfer devices; fresh water supply; fuel oil bunkers; workshop drawings; the regulations for the construction of the ship; and finally the ship's technical diary (according to Evers' book, *Kriegsschiffbau* [*Warship building*]). The diary contains important information on the ship, including her stability, speed and manoeuvrability, and keeps a record of the ship's history with notes on voyages, damage, alterations and repairs. All this is complemented by valid regulations, standing orders and special orders. The engineering officer takes care of the plans, although a number are also given to the section leader in charge.

All drawings are made in 1:100 scale, although a number of highly-detailed plans are as large as 1:10 scale. Because of their size, such drawings cannot be used for general service on board even by the personnel working in the appropriate sections such as engine room staff or damage control parties. Consequently another version of these plans and drawings are drawn in 1:200 scale and are accompanied by sketch booklets. These booklets, individually prepared for a particular section, contain diagrams of all installations and machinery employed in this section so that every sailor can quickly be trained for work.

Normal crew training on board a new ship begins during the construction period, when a few members of the key personnel attend the construction to supervise the installation of machinery and become acquainted with it. After commissioning, the on-board training commences with instruction on individual stations, and concludes with a muster. Following this comes training at sea, including action stations, and only when these have been completed is the ship ready for action.

Every warship is, according to its size, divided into numbered rooms, which facilitate duty on board and enable the individual to find his way when this number is announced on the public address system. The numeric system is based on the room distribution plan.

All data contained in the room distribution plan can also be found in the sketch booklets, in the annexes of which are copies of the general plans and design drawings. On the following page are examples of such schematic sketches.

Key: Roman numeral - section; first Arabic numeral - deck; second Arabic numeral - position on that particular deck.

Sections are counted from stern to bows. All rooms to starboard are numbered with odd numbers, while those to port bear even numbers. The numbers of rooms situated in the middle begin with the numeral 9.

The most important documents issued upon a ship's commission are the operating manuals, handbooks and regulations issued by the manufacturers of the installations, powerplants, machinery, pumps etc. Prior to their issue, these documents are examined and approved by the navy and given the status of official technical regulations. While these documents are the responsibility of the engineer officer, the handbooks and manuals are given to the section commanders. They are indispensable working aids for servicing and maintenance, but also for ordering spare parts. The schematic sectional drawing of a 15cm turret (below) is an example for such precise drawings which are available for all components of the armament of the ship. The documentation for technical sections is quite similar. The extract from one of the manuals, shown on the following pages, refers to a diesel engine for one of the ship's generators.

Sectional drawing of a battleship (schematic)

a armour belt
b splinter bulkhead
c torpedo bulkhead
d armoured upper deck
e main deck (armour deck)
f slope
1 double bottom 1
2 double bottom 2
3 outer terreplein
4 inner terreplein
5 stowing and lower platform deck
6 lower platform deck
7 upper platform deck
8 middle deck
9 main deck (armour deck)*
10 battery deck
11 upper deck
12 forecastle deck

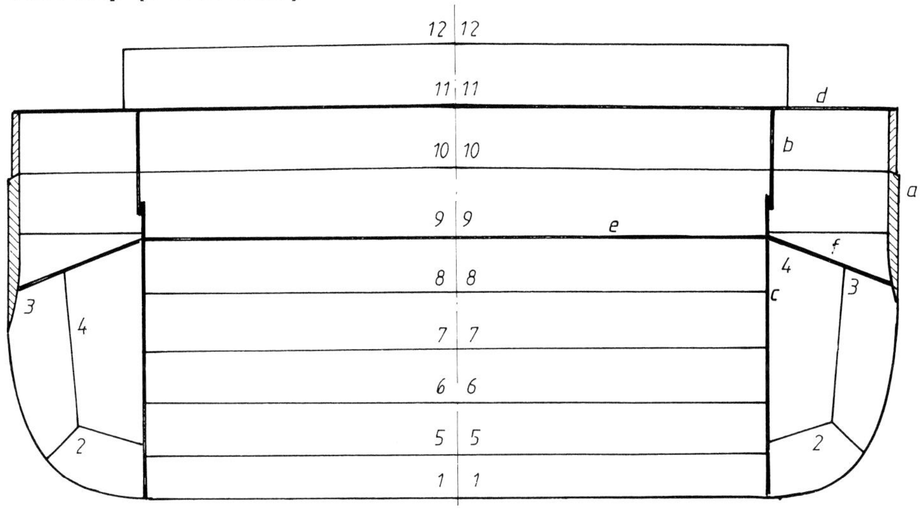

* On the *Bismarck*-class, the battery deck was also the armour deck.

Schematic room distribution within a compartment

Note:
In most cases, the stowing and the decks above are all in one room, for example the engine rooms, which can be several decks high.

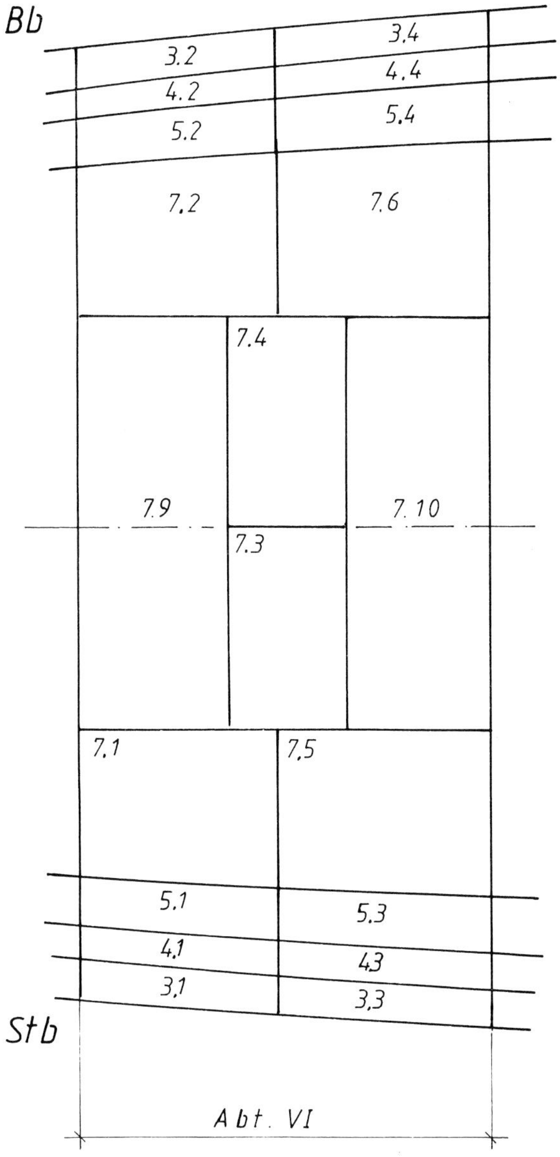

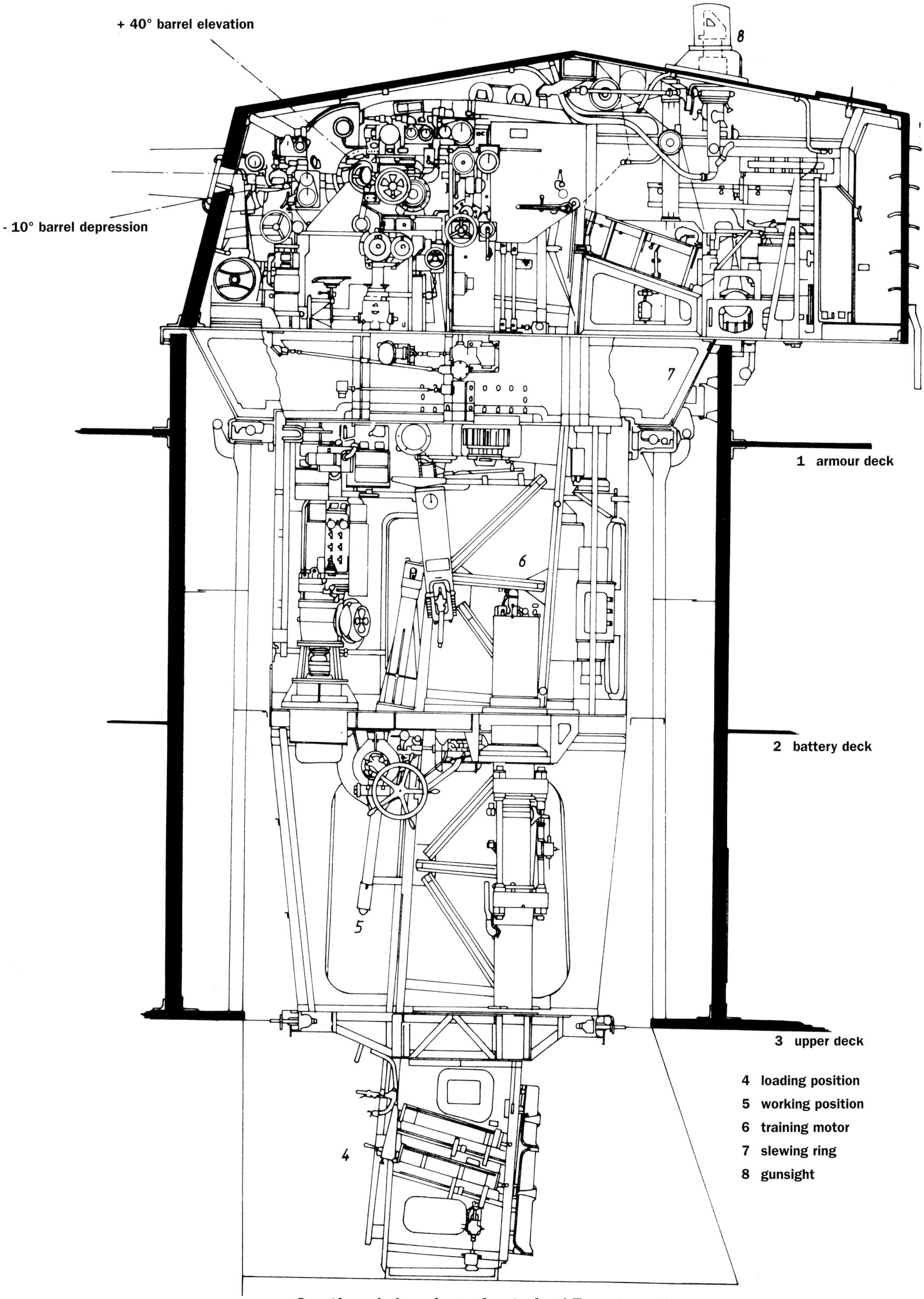

Sectional drawing of a twin 15cm turret on mounting C34 with 15cm guns C28

Original pages of the engineer's manual for one of the ship's large diesel engines, giving weights, measurements and manufacture numbers.

Ausfertigung

Nur für den Dienstgebrauch

Beschreibung und Betriebsvorschrift

für den

Dieselmotor RS 38 S

der Firma

MOTOREN-WERKE MANNHEIM A.-G.
VORM. BENZ ABT. STAT. MOTORENBAU
MANNHEIM

auf

Baujahr 1940

Die Übereinstimmung der Beschreibung und Betriebsvorschrift mit der Bauausführung bescheinigt:

Kriegsmarinewerft

, den 19

Marineoberbaurat

Für die militärische Ausbildung und Betriebsführung zugelassen:

Schiffsmaschineninspektion

, den 19

Beschreibung und Betriebsvorschrift | A. Bau- und Betriebsangaben | 1. Bauangaben | 1

A. Bau- und Betriebsangaben.

1. Bauangaben.

Hersteller des Dieselmotors: Motorenwerke Mannheim A.-G.
vorm. Benz Abt. Stat. Motorenbau
Mannheim

Fernruf: Mannheim 54121
Drahtanschrift: Alterbenz Mannheim

Bauart des Dieselmotors: RS 38 S

	Kreuzer „Seydlitz"	Schlachtschiff „Bismarck"	Schlachtschiff „Tirpitz"
Hersteller des Generators:	A. E. G.	Garbe-Lahmeyer	Garbe-Lahmeyer
Bauart des Generators:	G 84/38	P 23 FA 925 10 Spez. B 2	P 23 FA 925/10 + RP 91 sp.

Baunummer:

Schiff:	Motor Nr.	Generator Nr.	Aufstellungsort im Schiff
Kreuzer „Seydlitz"	42 885	534 576	E Werk 1
Schlachtschiff „Bismarck"	170 093	377 071	WE Masch. R 1
Schlachtschiff „Tirpitz"	170 094	376 848	WE Masch. R 1

Werkstoffe wichtiger Teile:

Gegenstand:	Lieferer:	Baustoff:	Festigkeitswerte
Triebwerkgehäuse	MWM	Stg. 45.81 u. St. 37.21	
Zylinderblock	MWM	Ge 26.91	
Laufbüchse	MWM	Spez.Ge.	
Arbeitskolben	Karl Schmidt GmbH., Neckarsulm	Spez.Al.Leg. KS 1275	
Kolbenringe	Friedr. Goetze Burscheid	Spez.Gußeisen	
Treibstange	MWM	VM 125	Bruchfest. = 65/80 kg/mm² Streckfestigkeit 65% Dehnung = 22/16% (l = 5d) Kerbzähigk. = 6/8 mkg/cm²
Kurbelwelle	MWM	S.M.St.	Bruchfest. 55/65 kg/mm² Streckfest. = 30/35 kg/mm² Dehnung = 19/18% Kerbzähigk = 4/5 mkg/cm² (D. V. M. Versuch)
Zylinderdeckel	MWM	Ge 26.91	
Anlaßluftleitung	MWM	Stahlrohr	

Beschreibung und Betriebsvorschrift | Werkstoffe wichtiger Teile | 2

Gegenstand:	Lieferer:	Baustoff:	Festigkeitswerte
Treibölleitung	MWM	Stahlrohr	
Motorenölleitung	MWM	Stahlrohr	
Kühlwasserleitung	MWM	Kupferrohr	
Abgassammelleitung	MWM	Gußeisen	
Rohre für Motoren-Oelkühler	Gerberich & Cie. Mannheim	Al-Ms (F 40/KM)	

Gewichte:

Gegenstand:	Kreuzer „Seydlitz"	Schlachtschiff „Bismarck"	Schlachtschiff „Tirpitz"
1 vollständiger Dieselmotor	ca. 7 000 kg	ca. 6 750 kg	ca. 6750 kg
Schwungrad	565 kg	230 kg	230 kg
Schwungradschutz	50 kg	35 kg	35 kg
Elastische Lagerung	950 kg	1 050 kg	1 050 kg
Anlaßluftbehälter vollständig	250 kg	250 kg	250 kg
Motorenölkühler	angebaut	260 kg	260 kg
Fundamentplatte	1 100 kg	1 465 kg	1 465 kg
Drehvorrichtung	33 kg	33 kg	33 kg
Generator	4 560 kg	7 360 kg	7 360 kg
Gesamtgewicht:	**14 508 kg**	**17 433 kg**	**17 433 kg**
Kühlwasser in Motor und Leitungen am Motor	250 kg	250 kg	250 kg
Motorenöl in Motor und Leitungen am Motor	80 kg	80 kg	80 kg

Diese Gewichte verstehen sich mit einem Spielraum von 5 v. Hundert.

Beschreibung und Betriebsvorschrift | A II. Hauptabmessungen | 3

Arbeitszylinder:
Zylinderzahl: 6
Durchmesser des Zylinders: 300 mm
Hub des Kolbens: 380 mm
Durchmesser der Kurbelwelle: 200 mm
Hubvolumen der Maschine: 162 Ltr.

Zündfolge:
für Linksmotor linksdrehend: 1 - 5 - 3 - 6 - 2 - 4

Einspritzventil:
Hersteller: Bosch
Bezeichnung: Düse DN 6 TD 50
Düsenhalter: KB 50 T 45 b
Durchmesser der Düsenlöcher: 2 mm
Lochzahl der Düse: 1

Einlaßventil:
Anzahl je Zylinder: 2 Stück
Durchmesser: 93 mm
Hub: 22,5 mm

Auslaßventil:
Anzahl je Zylinder: 2 Stück
Durchmesser: 93 mm
Hub: 22,5 mm

Sicherheitsventil:
Anzahl je Zylinder: 1 Stück
Durchmesser: 8 mm
Hub: 8 mm

Anlaßventil:
Anzahl je Zylinder: 1 Stück
Durchmesser: 34 mm
Hub: 6 mm

Arbeitskolben:
Hersteller: Karl Schmidt, Neckarsulm
Durchmesser: 300 mm
Länge: 470 mm
Entfernung Mitte Bolzen bis Oberkante: 240 mm
Anzahl der Kolbenringe: 6 Stück
Anzahl der Oelabstreifringe: 1 Stück

Zylinderbüchse:
Länge: 810 mm

Lager:

	Durchmesser	Länge
Hauptlager:	200 mm	115 mm
Paßlager:	200 mm	155 mm
Kurbelzapfenlager:	200 mm	138 mm
Kolbenbolzenlager:	120 mm	130 mm

Beschreibung und Betriebsvorschrift	A III. Betriebsangaben	6

A III Betriebsangaben:

Drehzahlen:

Schiff		Kreuzer „Seydlitz"	Schlachtschiff „Bismarck"	Schlachtschiff „Tirpitz"
Baunummer der Maschine		42 885	170 093	170 094
Betriebszahl bei Normal und Ueberlast	n/min.	600	600	600
Sicherheitsregler stellt Maschine ab bei	n/min.	ca. 660	ca. 660	ca. 660
entsprechend einer Reglerdrehzahl von	n/min.	2900	3040	3040
kritisches Drehzahlgebiet ηe I von/bis	n/min.	440/470	480/580	480/580
kritisches Drehzahlgebiet ηe II von/bis	n/min	660/730	700/720	700/720
Schwingungsfrequenzen ηe I	n/min.	4150	3200	3200

Betriebsdrücke:

Abspritzdruck des Einspritzventils:		etwa 110 atü
Verdichtungsdruck:		etwa 45 atü
Zünddruck:		etwa 60 atü
Abblasedruck des Sicherheitsventils im Zylinderdeckel:		80 atü
Anlaßluftbehälter, Höchstdruck:		60 atü
Zum Anlassen erforderlicher Mindestdruck:		12 atü
Motorenöl-Höchstdruck vor dem Filter:	bei warmer Maschine	5,5 atü
Motorenöl-Höchstdruck hinter dem Filter:	bei warmer Maschine	3,5 atü
Motorenöl - niedrigster Oeldruck hinter dem Filter:	bei warmer Maschine	1,5 atü
Motorenöl - höchster Oeldruck vor dem Filter, bei kalter Maschine:		8,0 atü
Kühlwasser-Abblasedruck des Sicherheitsventils an der Pumpe:		5,0 atü

Probedrücke:

Kühlwasserraum im Zylinderblock:	6 atü
Kühlwasserraum im Zylinderdeckel:	15 atü
Anlaßluftbehälter:	90 atü

Beschreibung und Betriebsvorschrift	A III. Betriebsangaben	9

A IV. Leistungsangaben:

Schiff	Anzahl der Motoren	Motor-Nr	Normallast		20% Überlast Dauer 30 Min		mittl. effekt. Druck pe kg/cm²	mittl. Kolben Geschw. Vm m/s	Literleistung PSe/Ltr.
			n/min.	PSe	Drehzahl n/min.	Leistung PSe			
Kreuzer „Seydlitz"	1	42885	600	525	600	630	4,85	7,6	3,24
Schlachtschiff „Bismarck"	1	170093	600	460	600	550	4,25	7,6	2,84
Schlachtschiff „Tirpitz"	1	170094	600	460	600	550	4,25	7,6	2,84

Die auf dem Prüfstand der MWM erzielten für Leistung, mittleren effektiven Druck und die zugehörigen Abgastemperaturen sind für alle Belastungen auf dem anhängenden Schaubild Abb. 46 und 47 eingetragen.

A view of the diesel engine for one of the ship's generators.

Beschreibung und Betriebsvorschrift	**Motorzusammenstellung** **Querschnitt des Motors und Ansicht auf Bedienungsstand** nur für Schlachtschiff „Bismarck" und „Tirpitz"	**Abb. 1**

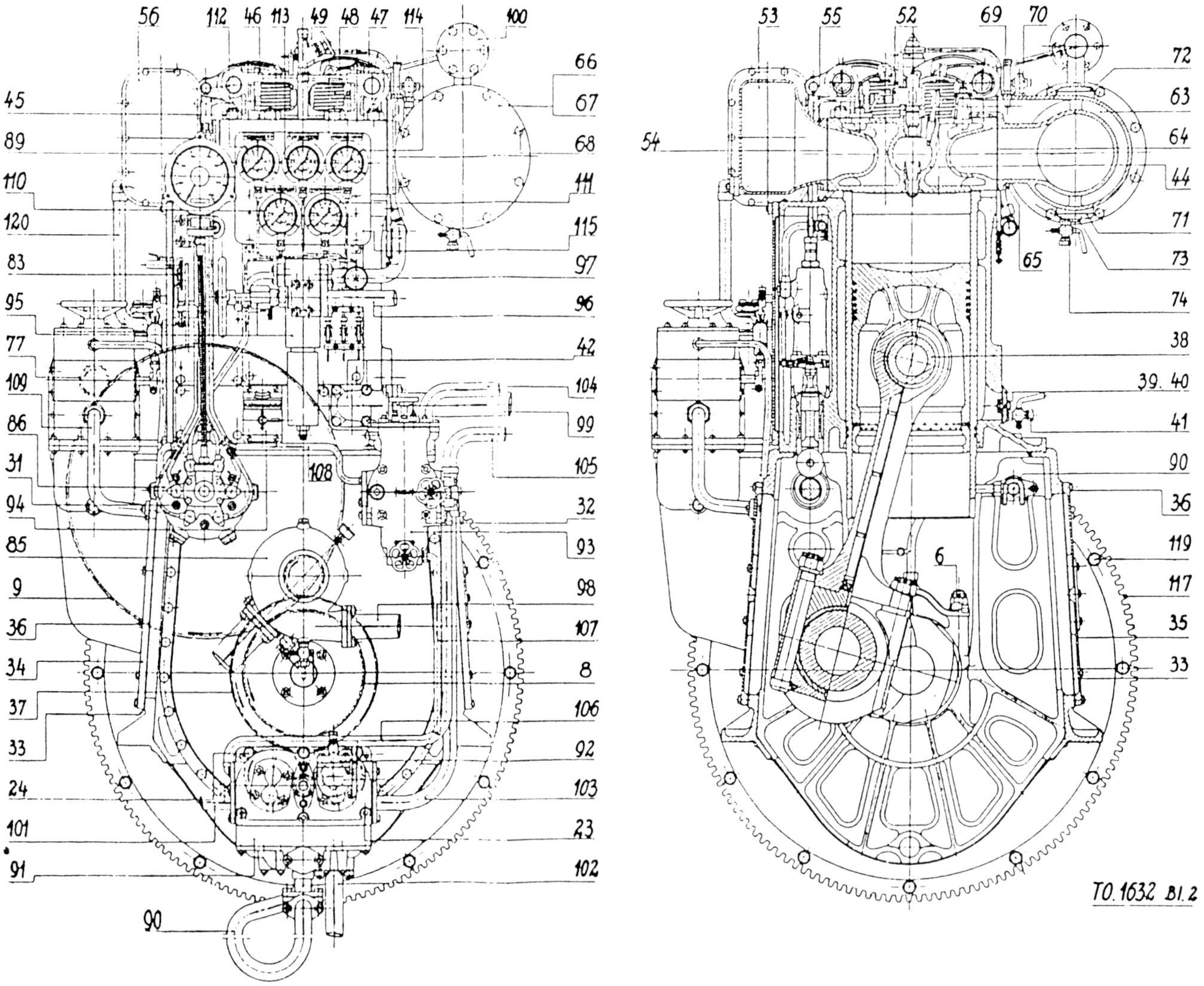

Sectional view of the motor and view of the operating panel for battleships *Bismarck* and *Tirpitz* only

6 studs with castle nuts, cotter pin and locking plate
8 two-piece spur gear, on crankshaft
9 spur gear on camshaft, see fig 14
23 hexagonal head nut and bolt
24 hexagonal bolt
31 collar bolt with hexagonal nut
32 collar bolt with hexagonal nut
33 gasket
34 cover
35 cover
36 hexagonal bolt
37 spur gear for oil pump drive
38 motor block, see fig 12
39 flange, zinc-protected, with gasket
40 hexagonal bolt
41 straight-way cock with gasket
42 water inlet manifold with gasket and hexagonal bolt
44 rocker cover
45 stud with hexagonal nut
46 valve rocker with block, see fig 16
47 stud with castle nut and cotter pin
49 indication valve with seals
52 injection valve, see fig 8
53 inlet manifold
54 gasket
55 hexagonal nut
56 blank-off flange
63 tail pipe
64 gasket
65 hexagonal bolt
66 round gasket
67 blank-off flange
68 hexagonal head nut and bolt
69 exhaust temperature indicator with gasket
70 sealing ring with pet cock
71 zinc-protected flange
72 gasket
73 hexagonal bolt
74 straight-way cock with gasket
77 govenor drive gear
83 fuel shutdown device with indicator
85 coolant rotary pump, see fig 35
86 compressed starter-air distributer, see fig 27
89 tachometer
90 lubrication oil lines, see fig 30
91 oil pump, see fig 32
92 fuel pump, see fig 22
93 oil filter, see fig 32
94 heater plug switch
95 pressure reduction- and stop valve, see fig 26
96 starting air lines from compressed air cylinder
97 starting air lines, see fig 25
98 coolant lines to oil cooler
99 coolant lines from oil cooler
100 coolant collection line
101 pressure line of the oil pump to the oil reservoir
102 pressure line of the oil pump from the oil reservoir
103 from pump to oil filter
104 from oil filter to oil cooler
105 from oil cooler through oil filter to oil distribution line inside the motor block
106 engine oil overflow from oil regulation valve to oil supply line
107 sludge outlet
108 oil pressure line to hydraulic regulator
109 backflow line from hydraulic regulator to motor block
110 pressure gauge with line, for starting air pressure
111 pressure gauge with line, for pressure of compressed air cylinder
112 pressure gauge with line, for coolant
113 pressure gauge with line, in front of filter
114 pressure gauge with line, behind filter
115 pressure gauges panel
117 rack
119 hexagonal nut with locking plate
120 air vent tube

Beschreibung und Betriebsvorschrift	**Motorzusammenstellung** **Längsansicht des Motors** nur für Schlachtschiff „Bismarck" und „Tirpitz"	**Abb. 2**

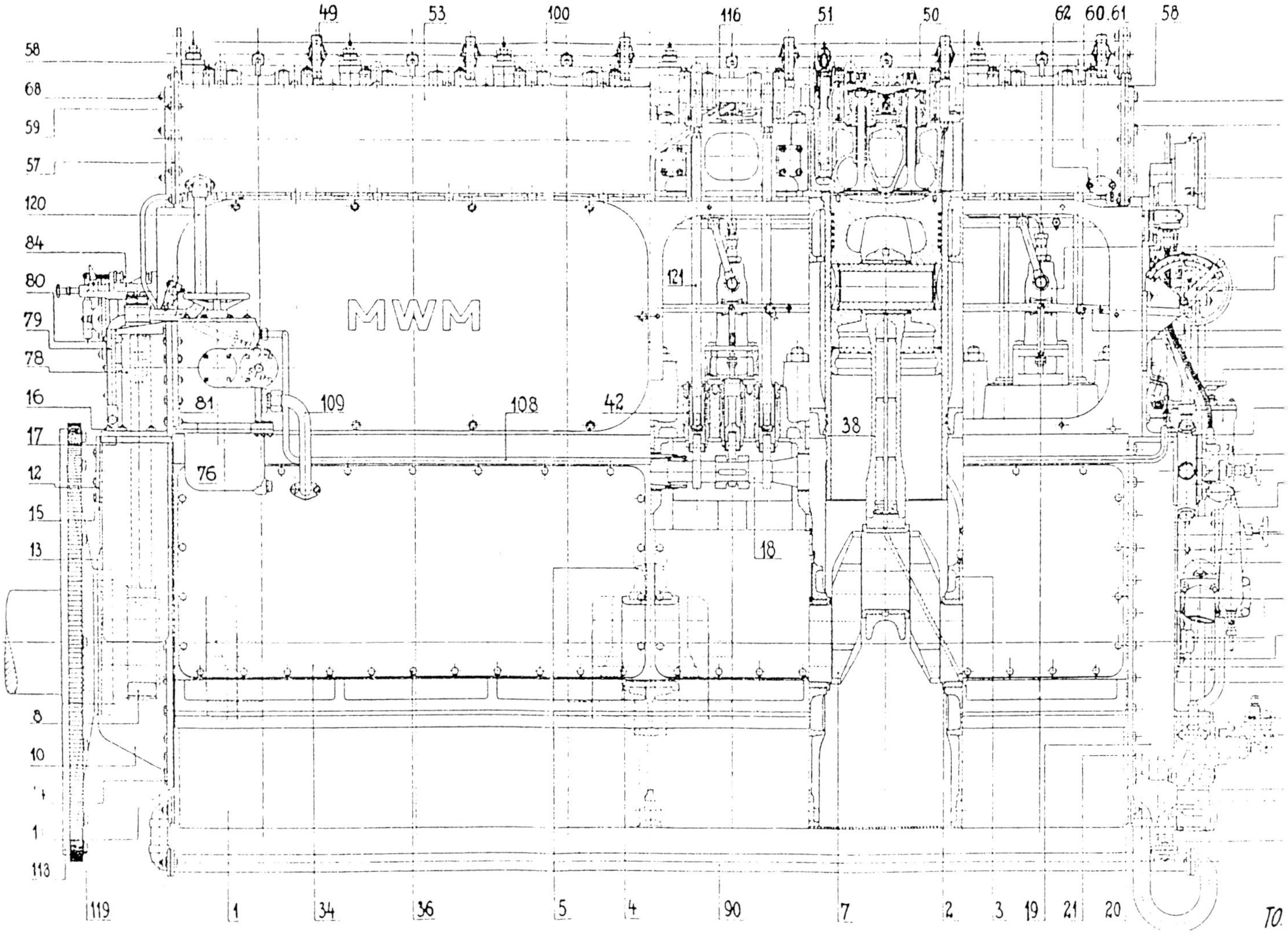

1 motor housing
2 main bearings
3 bearing cover with lubrication nipple and gasket
4 bearing shells
5 bearing cover with lubrication nipple and gasket
6 studs with castle nuts, cotter pin and locking plate
7 crankshaft
8 two-piece spur gear, on crankshaft
9 spur gear on camshaft, see fig 14
10 front cover
11 gasket
12 cover
13 gasket
14 hexagonal bolt
15 hexagonal bolt
16 studs with castle nut
17 gasket
18 camshaft, complete, see fig 14
19 front cover
20 gasket
21 hexagonal bolt
22 gasket
23 hexagonal nut and bolt
25 O-ring seal
26 cover
27 collar bolt with hexagonal nut
28 castle nut
29 collar bolt with hexagonal nut
30 O-ring seal
32 collar bolt with hexagonal nut
34 cover
36 hexagonal bolt
38 motor block, see fig 12
42 water inlet manifold with gasket and hexagonal bolt
49 indicator valve with seals
50 inlet- and oulet valve, see fig 6
51 starter valve, see fig 10
53 intake pipe
56 blank-off flange
57 connecting flange
58 gasket
59 hexagonal nut and bolt
60 oval blank-off flange
61 oval gasket
62 collar bolt with hexagonal nut
68 hexagonal nut and bolt
75 fuel injection pump, see fig 24
76 hydraulic regulator, see fig 17
78 regulator housing
79 blank-off flange with gasket
80 collar bolt with hexagonal nut
81 hexagonal nut and bolt
82 govenor control linkage, see fig 20
83 fuel cut-off with indicator
84 safety regulator, see fig 19
85 coolant rotary pump, see fig 35
86 compressed starter-air distributer, see fig 27
87 tachometer drive gear, see fig 40
88 flexible shaft
89 tachometer
90 motor oil line, see fig 30
91 oil pump, see fig 32
92 fuel pump, see fig 22
93 oil filter, see fig 31
100 coolant collection line, see fig 36
108 pressure line to hydraulic regulator
109 pressure line from hydraulic regulator to motor housing
116 fuel supply line
117 rack
119 hexagonal nut with locking plate
120 air vent tube

Detailed plans of the ship's large diesel engines from the original engineer's manual.

Career notes

1936: 2 November, ship's keel laid at the *Kriegsmarinewerft*, Wilhelmshaven .

1939: 1 April, launch.

1941: 25 February, *Tirpitz* commissioned. After acceptance trials in March, she transferred to the Baltic Sea. Working-up periods at Kiel and Gotenhafen, accelerated training of the crew and trials in order to provide full action readiness. As this could not be achieved before mid-May 1941 her planned participation in Operation Rheinübung was not realized. In September she had a brief employment with the *Baltenflotte* 'Baltic fleet'.

1942: Returned to the North Sea in mid-January, final fitting at Wilhelmshaven-Reede and transferred to Norway. In March she took part in an unsuccessful operation against allied convoys, during which she was exposed to permanent Allied air attacks. Her main berths were the Faettenfjord near Drontheim and the Altafjord. In July there was a further attempt to attack convoys but *Tirpitz* was then transferred to a new berth in the Bogen bay near Narvik. Returned to Faettenfjord for repairs in the shipyard.

1943: Returned to Bogen Bay and then to Kaafjord. In September she was part of Operation Sizilien, the bombardment of Spitzbergen. This was the only time she fired her heavy artillery in anger, even though it was not during an action at sea. In the same month the British managed to attack the ship with miniature submarines which put her out of action for some time.

1944: This year was marked by enforced Allied efforts to put the ship out of action by incessant air attacks. Beginning in April, these attacks were continuously launched, but many sorties had to be aborted or cancelled due to rapidly changing weather conditions. They were, however, not without results. On 3 April there was a first successful heavy attack, and another attack on 15 September caused so much damage that she was no longer seaworthy. *Tirpitz* was ordered to transfer to Tromsö, where she was to remain as a floating battery. Another air attack on 29 October caused serious damage, and then, on 12 November, came the end. Hit by superheavy bombs, the ship capsized, with over 1,200 men lost.

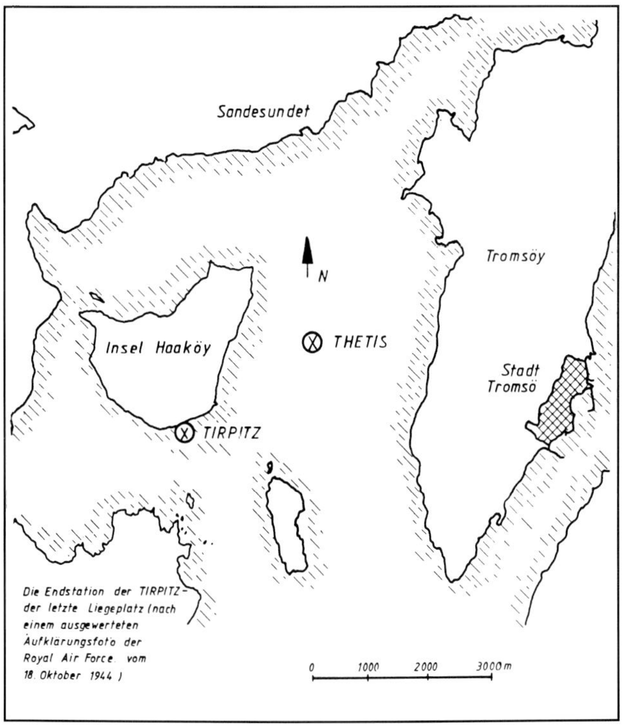

The site where *Tirpitz* capsized.

The wreck of *Tirpitz,* after the first attempts of breaking up the ship. In the foreground one of the mighty craters caused by the air attack can be seen.

This photograph shows a diesel engine of the RS 38S type which was used on both *Tirpitz* and *Bismarck.* A twelve-cylinder variant with the designation RS 38Zw, based on this engine, was later employed in submarines of the XI-class.

▶
An aerial view of building slip 2 of the *Kriegsmarinewerft* 'Navy shipyard' in Wilhelmshaven. The hull of the new battleship is still under construction. Note the many transverse frames and the bulkheads which have already been fitted. On the right and left the stagings can be seen.

A starboard view of the ship under construction. The armour deck has been completed, and the cylindrical supports of the barbettes for the 15cm turrets and of 38cm turret A have also been installed.

The launch of *Tirpitz* on 1 April 1939. Hitler and his companions pass the guard of honour on their way to the platform.

As can be seen here a large number of spectators attended the launch.

The new ship just before the naming ceremony. Seen at the port bow is one of the anchors intended to stop the ship after the launch and to turn her out of the launching direction.

After the naming ceremony, the guests leave the tribune.

A photo of *Tirpitz* prior to her launch which affords a good view of the tilting sledge and the front console.

The massive hull slips slowly into the water affording a good view of the front anchor and large brake shields.

The hull has now been turned around and tugged to the Bauhafen-basin, where she is moored near the drydocks IV, V and VI. The battleship *Scharnhorst* is moored at the eastern quay.

Taken in the winter of 1940/41, this photograph shows *Tirpitz* on the southern quay of the Navy shipyard during the working-up period. The funnel and bridge tower have been completed although some of the platforms are still under construction. The searchlights have already been fitted to the funnel platform, and to the right of the bridge tower, the fore AA-artillery director control tower can be seen. The boats are already on board. The turrets of her main and secondary armament are complete and the twin mountings of the 10.5cm AA guns have been fitted.

Tirpitz during the fitting-out period, in 1940. The two 15cm turrets Stb II and Stb III can be seen, the latter still missing its rangefinder. The starboard hangar on its right is still under construction and on the after deck many covered openings can be seen, including the barbettes for the turrets C and D. Premanufactured barrings for the ship's boats have been fitted to the side of the hangar. In the background are slips I and II, and dry docks I, II and III on which a large new construction can be seen (probably the light cruiser *N* which was later broken up).

Tirpitz during her fitting-out period, moored at the eastern quay of the construction harbour. Note the camouflage pattern which resembles wooden shacks with windows.

Another view of the ship from a different angle. The paintwork on the ship seems to be quite realistic.

View from the bridge onto the forecastle. Turret A has been trained to starboard, while turret B is still in its basic position. On the platform in the foreground, one of the many single 2cm AA guns is visible. The fore armoured conning tower can be seen on the front part of the bridge superstructure. Its revolving hood with the 7m base rangefinder and the aerial of the radar set FuMO 23 attached to it has also been trained to starboard. This photograph dates from the summer of 1941.

Tirpitz in the Baltic, November 1941. Turret C has just fired a salvo, thick fumes cover parts of the ship.

Tirpitz in the Baltic, Summer 1941. At this time, many propaganda films or photographs were taken. This was either done with a camera on board the ship or, as shown here, with the camera in one of the ship's aircraft which then circled the ship. Turret A has been trained to starboard.

The Aradao Ar 196 during the shooting. Turret A has again been trained to starboard; on its roof and on the upper deck many spectators can be seen.

Here, one of the cameramen can be seen operating his camera on a tripod placed in one of the boats.

Tirpitz in the Baltic in 1941, a view from her bows. In the foreground are the two heavy 38cm turrets A and B with capstans in front. Note that the barrel ports on the front of the turrets have been closed with canvas hoods to protect the turrets from spray and water. This was important as water inside the turret could cause malfunctions. The wings of the bridge have been folded down and the revolving hoods on the conning tower and foretop have been turned aft. This was common practice in order to hide certain parts of the ship from view; here the large radar aerials are being hidden.

A view of the forecastle. Turret A has been trained to starboard, while turret B has been trained to port. Note that turret A is not equipped with a rangefinder. As the gun ports in the turrets are covered with canvas bags the action shown here is possibly normal training or maintenance.

Meeting with a submarine of the II class. The port aircraft crane, one of the 10.5cm AA guns and also the 15cm turret Bb II with its 6.5m base rangefinder are all visible.

The Baltic in 1941, gymnastics at the bar. Physical training was taken very seriously in the German Navy, and there were many different kinds of sports, although the wearing of appropriate attire was of secondary importance.

The Baltic in 1941 with 15cm turrets Stb I and II visible. The ship's band is playing as part of leisure time on board. There were precise regulations for leisure time both in peace and wartime, particularly as far as the ship's upper deck was concerned: there were separate areas for the different ranks. All regulations were laid down in the M D V Nr49 (regulations for the navy), D a B *Dienst an Bord* 'Service on Board', volume II, derived from the former *Instruktionen for den Commandanten eines Seiner Majestät Schiffes oder Fahrzeuges* 'Instructions for the Commandant of one of His Majesty's Ships or Vessels', dated 1852 and 1853, 1872 and 1877. Further revised and modernised versions were published in 1894, 1903, 1909, 1925 and 1937.
The D a B consisted of five volumes:
I: Rights and duties of the ship's commandant, regulations for the ship's officers and regulations for ensigns, petty officers etc.
II: Service on board.
III: Regulations for guard and security duties.
IV: Regulations for the employment of the ship such as orders for the conduct of the ship, for sailing in foreign waters, for the political activities of the commandants of German ships abroad, and for the relations between warships and merchant ships in times of war and peace.
V: Regulations for the commissioning and the service of the ship, her equipment, paying-off of the ship and for changes of command or changes of the crew.
There were special regulations for subjects such as tactics, organisation, administration, weapons, machinery and health care.

The Baltic in 1941, training of the ship's crew. Here the sailors are seen doing anchor drill.

Starboard view of turret B, turret Stb I and the bridge superstructure including the bridge tower. Typically in photographs of this era, the revolving hoods of the fore director control tower and foretop have been trained aft in order to hide the large radar aerials from view.

Summer 1942, a view of the starboard superstructure near the funnel and just behind the bridge tower.

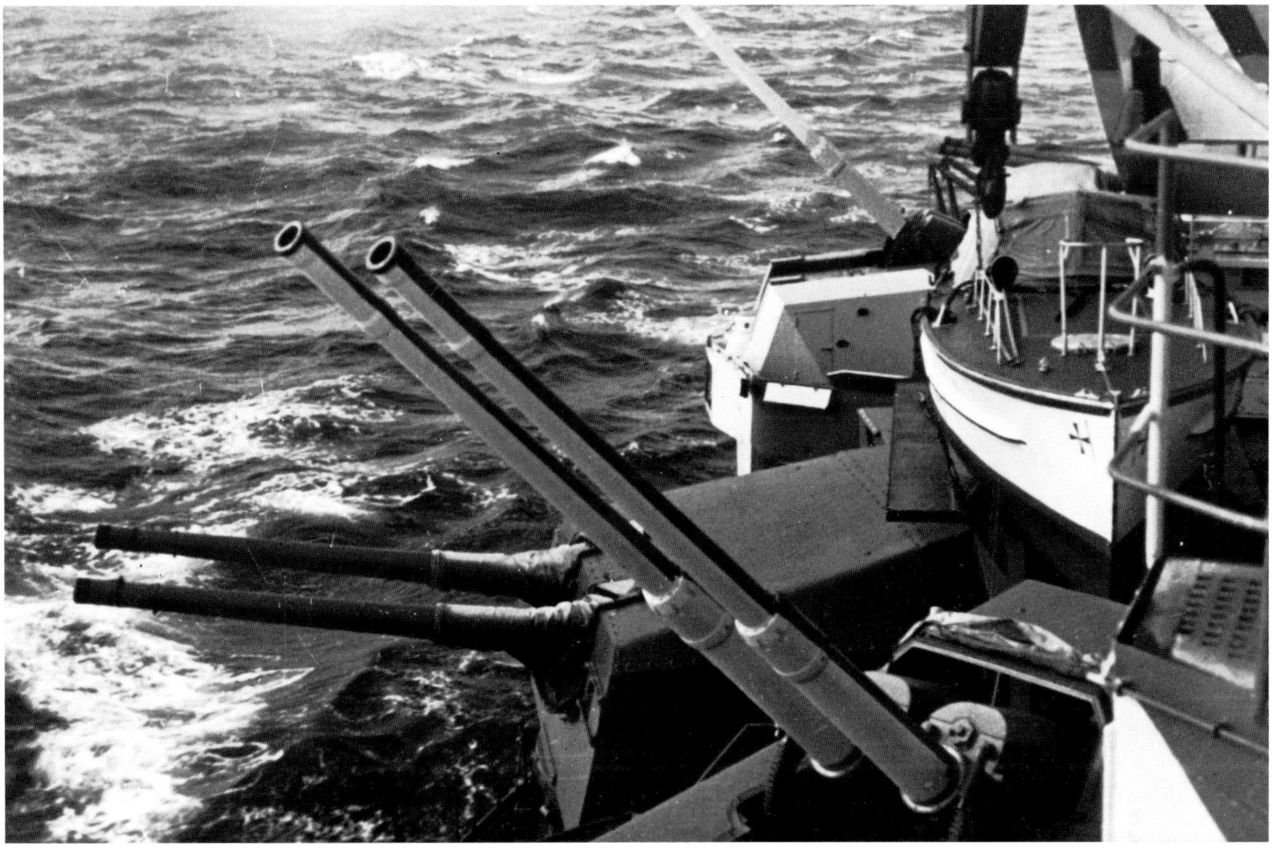

View of the two starboard 10.5cm AA guns in twin mountings and the 15cm turret Stb II. On the right is a pinnace with the Admiral's pennant on the bow. Note the camouflage patterns applied to the guns.

View from the foretop onto the quarterdeck. In the foreground the funnel with the gas outlets can be seen, with the single pole of the mainmast directly behind. Behind the mainmast itself is the aft director control tower for the ship's AA artillery. Turrets C and D have been trained to port and starboard respectively. Also note the 15cm turret Bb III and the 10.5cm AA gun in twin mounting.

Tirpitz approaching the Lofoten islands, 9 March 1942. The 10.5cm AA guns are manned, as are the lighter weapons.

Tirpitz in Norway, 1943. This is a view from the forecastle. Note, in the foreground, stairs have been fitted to the breakwater which is rather high and difficult to traverse. The breakwater had to split breaking seas in order to protect delicate parts of the ship from the force of the water. The front part of the bridge superstructure, with handrails and step irons attached, can be seen to the right of the frame. The two 15cm turrets Stb I and II are in their basic positions and the barrels of the twin 10.5cm AA guns are elevated towards the sky.

◀ *Tirpitz* in 1944. The revolving hood on the foretop with the 10.5m base rangefinder is fitted with additional platforms; the hood already carries the new aerial of the radar set FuMO 26. Turret B has been trained to starboard, and the revolving hood of the fore conning tower with the aerial of the FuMO 23 has also been trained to this direction. Both wings of the bridge have been folded up. Note the swastika in the white roundel on the forecastle which served as an aerial recognition aid.

Tirpitz in 1943. A view of the bridge tower. The two revolving hoods on the foretop have been trained aft which affords a good view of the 10.5m base rangefinder and the aerials of the radar sets FuMO 23 and FuMO 27. The two round cupolas are the hoods of the fore AA artillery director control towers.

A view from the bridge tower onto the forecastle. The 2cm AA guns in quadruple mounting fitted in 1942 to the roof of turret B and the bridge superstructure are visible. ▶

Tirpitz in 1944. Note the new aerial of the FuMO 26 radar in the foretop. A number of vessels are moored to her sides which suggests that the ship is probably being repaired after suffering battle damage.

One of the many 2cm AA guns in quadruple mounting. The weapon was quite efficient in close-range fighting, but there was no protection for the guncrews from attacking low-flying aircraft which had managed to break through the screen of defensive fire.

Dating from 1942 this photograph gives a view of bridge tower and funnel. The foretop has been fitted with an additional observation platform and the revolving hood has been fitted with another radar aerial of the FuMo 27-type, in addition to the aerial of the FuMo 23.

Camouflage Schemes

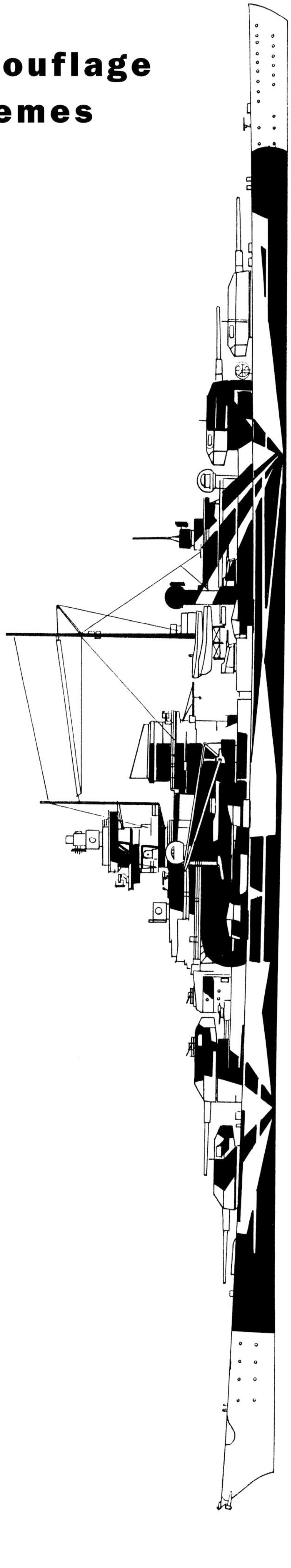

Camouflage pattern July 1942, port side

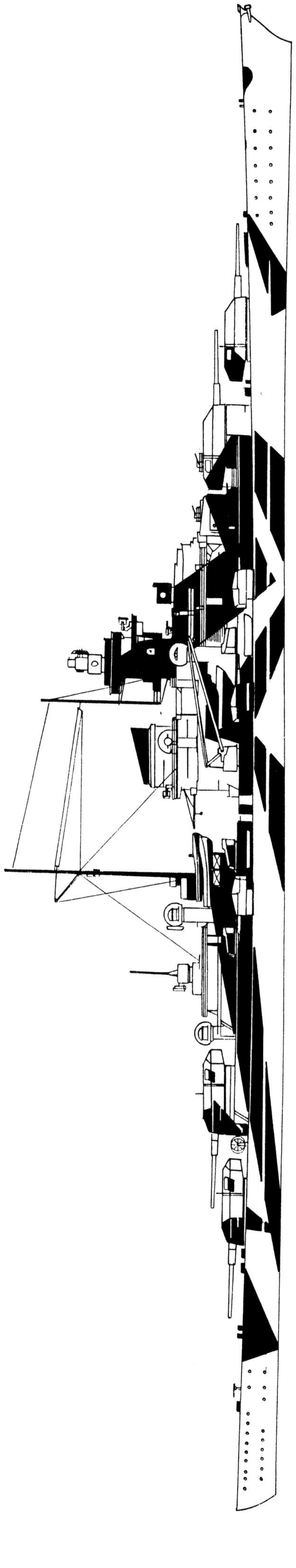

Camouflage pattern March 1944, starboard side

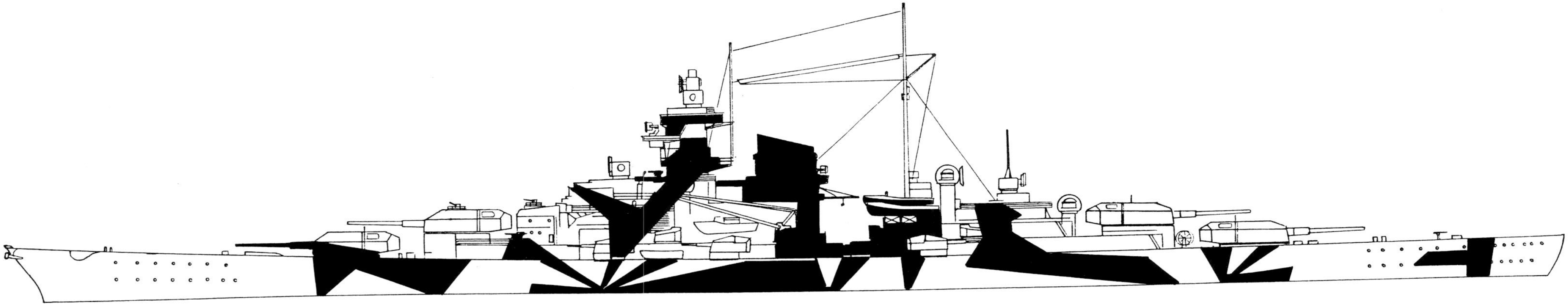

Camouflage pattern March 1944, port side

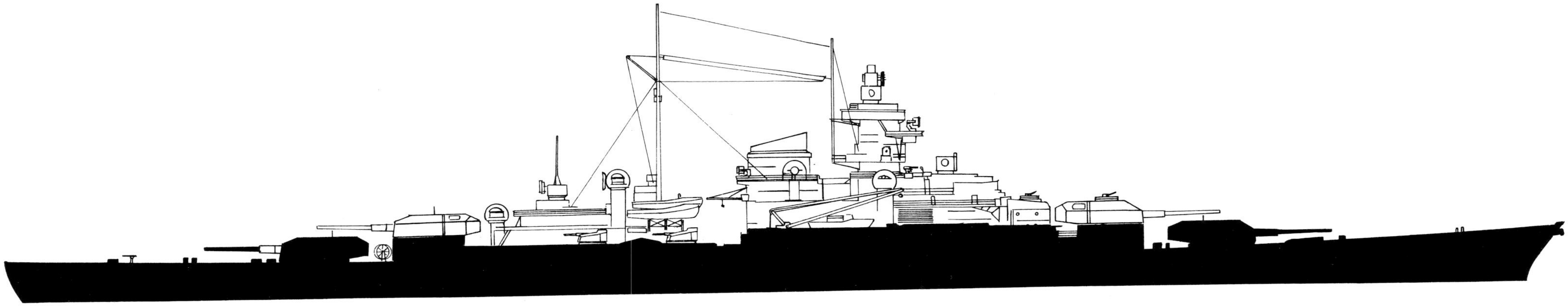

Camouflage pattern May - August 1944, starboard side

Tirpitz as scale model

This model of *Tirpitz*, built in 1:100 scale by Mr W Fraider, is on display in the Kuestenmuseum in Wilhelmshaven. It belongs to a series of German warship models, all built in the same scale by the same modeller, depicting ships from the early German navies to the Kriegsmarine in 1945.

As this model of *Tirpitz* was fairly expensive, many societies and institutions and also the Bordgemeinschaft Tirpitz (a society of ex-sailors who sailed on *Tirpitz* and who have annual meetings in Wilhelmshaven) made collections and donated this model to the museum.

A complete view of the model showing *Tirpitz* as she appeared in 1943-4.

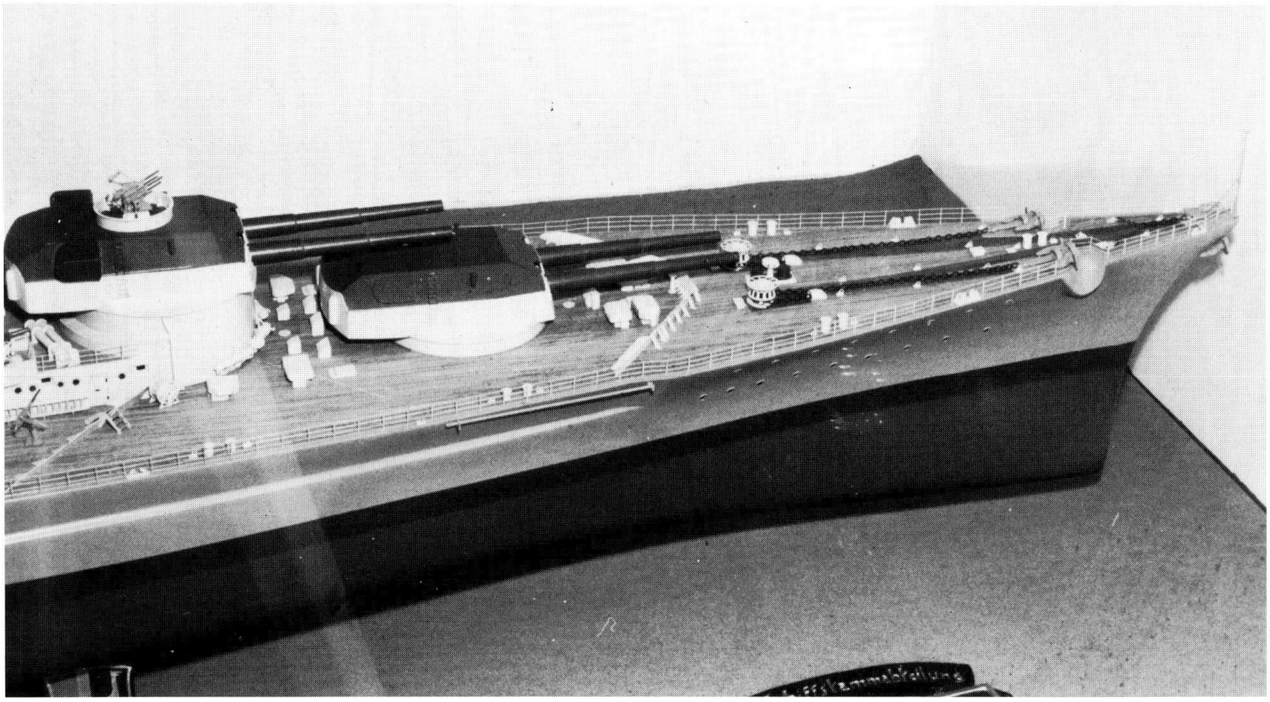

The front of the model. On top of turret B there is a 2cm AA gun in quadruple mounting, and behind the barbette another 2cm AA gun in single mounting. The eye anchor is at the bow and the other two anchors can be seen in the hawses on starboard and port. Note the many hatches and caps on the upper deck including cable and line drums and also capstans. On the ship's side beneath the fore breakwater is the starboard boom in its folded-down position.

Bridge, conning tower, bridge tower and funnel. Note the 2cm AA gun in quadruple mounting on turret B and another one behind this turret on the bridge. An additional gun mounting can be seen on the platform under the foretop platform, with a searchlight behind. There are many 3.7cm AA guns in twin mountings on the far side of turret B and on the deck behind the conning tower. On the foretop the original revolving hood with the 10.5m base rangefinder can be seen. Two additional platforms have now been fitted, and the revolving hood carries the aerials for the radar sets FuMO 23 and FuMO 27. The director control towers for the fore twin 10.5cm AA guns are covered with round hoods. There is another quadruple 2cm AA gun, and a searchlight, on the funnel platform. The two 15cm turrets Stb I and Stb II and also the twin 10.5cm AA guns can be seen on the upper deck. The starboard crane is in its basic position; the boats are stowed between this and the funnel.

The midship section. The mainmast stands on top of the hangar, and on the far aft side are the cupolas of the two aft AA artillery director control towers. Between them is the aft conning tower with its 10.5m base rangefinder and two more 2cm AA guns in twin mountings. The catapult is mounted in a transverse position between mainmast and funnel, and it carries an Arado Ar 196. Directly behind and under the catapult a number of torpedo tubes can be seen; these were added when the ship was planned as a commerce raider in the Atlantic. *Tirpitz* never took on this role as *Bismarck* was sunk. Behind the catapult is 15cm turret Stb III, and above it two more twin 10.5cm AA guns. Note the bilge keel at the hull. The model visible behind *Tirpitz* is the pocket battleship *Admiral Graf Spee.*

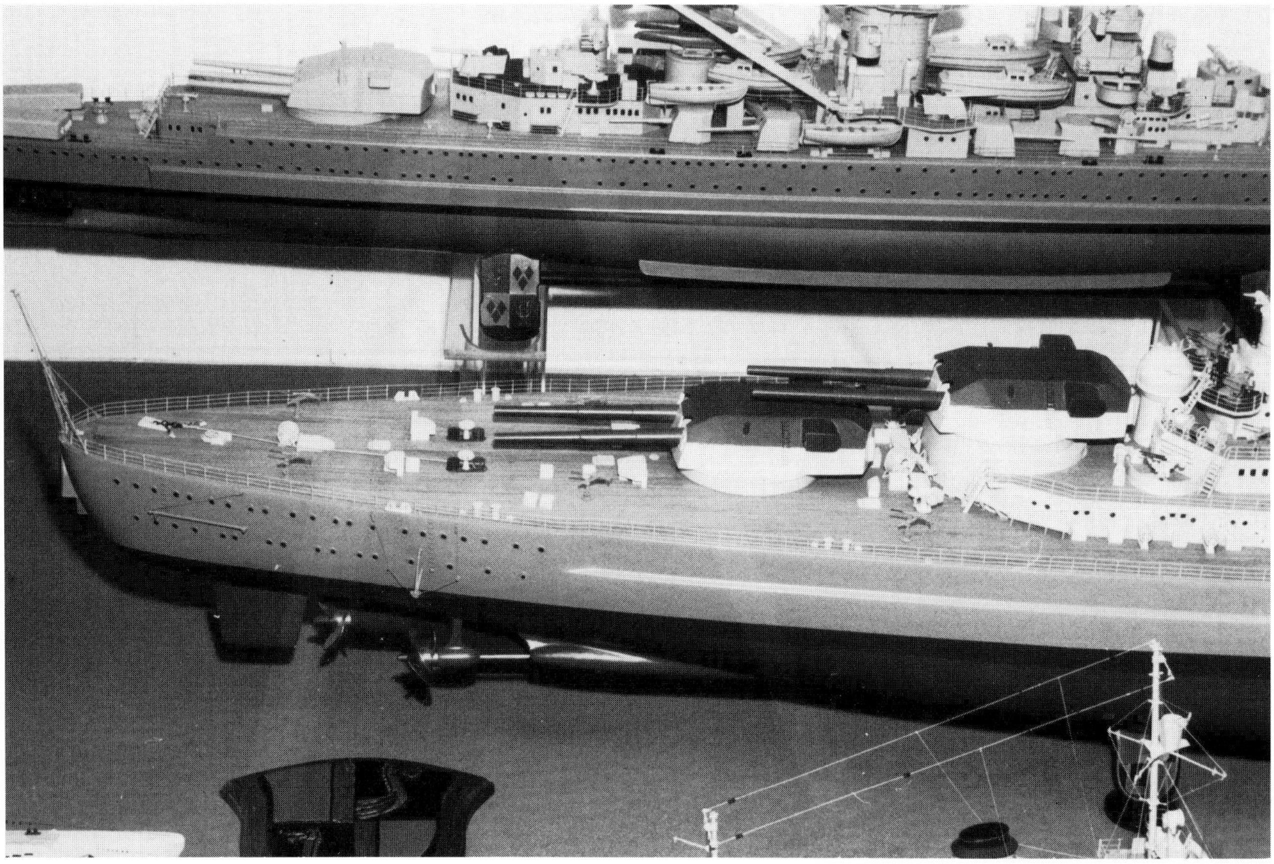

Shown here are the stern of *Tirpitz* and the two after turrets C and D. Also visible are the 2cm AA guns in single mountings on the deck directly behind turret C and a 3.7cm AA gun in twin mounting. Note the stern anchor, the arrangement of the propellers and rudders and also the many reels and hatches on the deck.

Another view of the rear part of the ship. Note the numerous superstructures and hatches on the upper deck. No rope reel, cable reel, companion hatch, bollard or railing post has been forgotten. The model in the background is the pocket battleship *Admiral Graf Spee.*

Another view of the midship section, seen from a different angle. Note the edge of the armour belt visible on the side of the hull.

Bridge superstructure, bridge tower and funnel seen from an upper perspective. It is amazing to find out how many details can be seen on a model of this size, many more details than on a real ship. Photographs of a real ship usually show her in action while on a model everything is in its basic position. Note the two wings of the bridges which are folded down. In front of the barbette of turret B, the Otter devices of the mine-clearing gear can be seen. The small caps on top of the conning tower are periscopes and aiming devices.

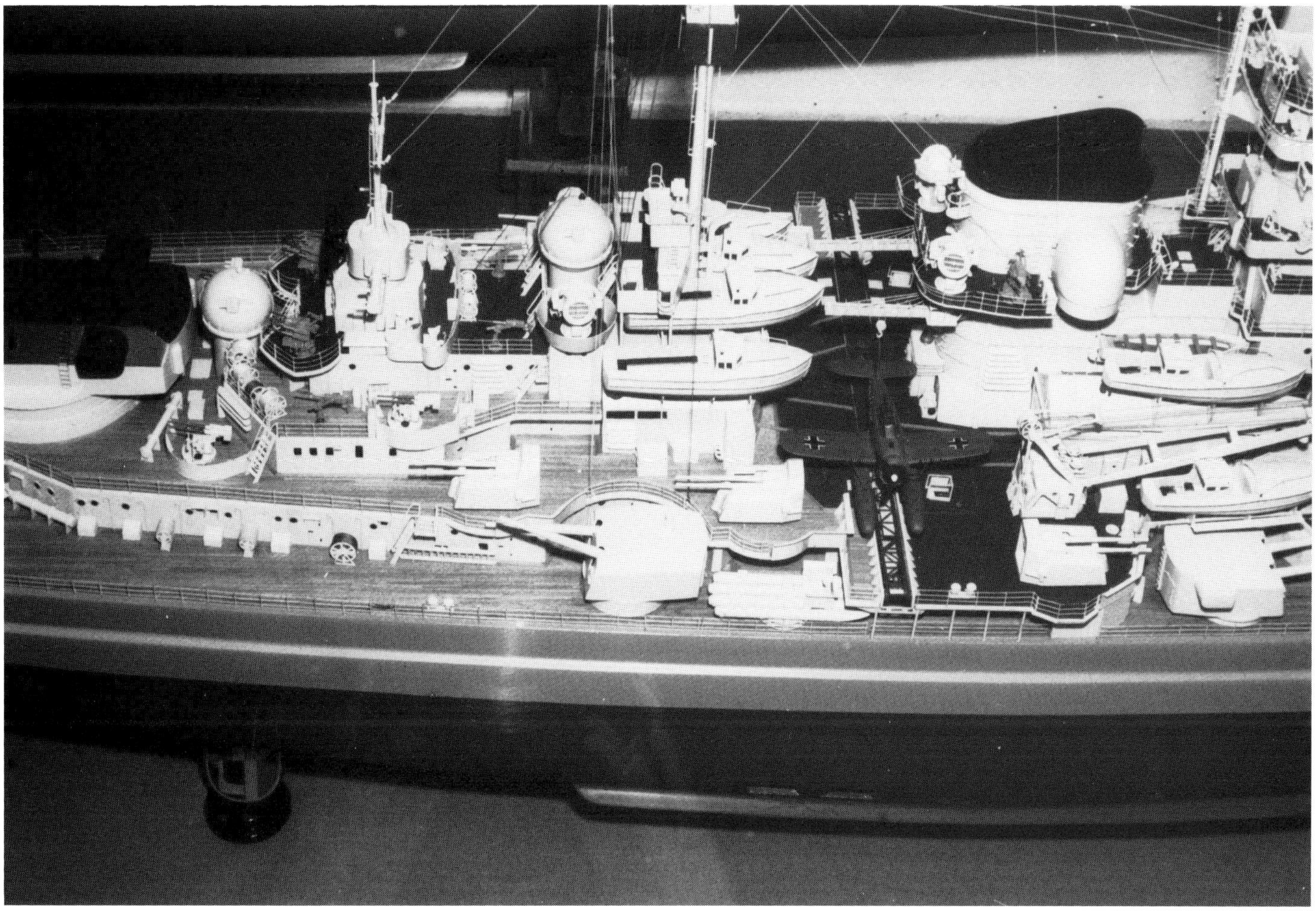

Another four photographs taken from a variety of angles with detailed views of the different sections of the deck superstructure. Note the various types of boats.

The model of *Tirpitz* seen from behind. Above the starboard propeller the folded-up propeller protector can be seen, and behind it the boom at the stern. Note the taper of the armour belt. Behind *Tirpitz* is the model of *Admiral Graf Spee*, and in the foreground a model of a type M40 minesweeper.

A radio-controlled model of *Tirpitz* built by Mr R Wagner from Nordholz/Cuxhaven in Germany.

The plans

Plan 01 Internal profile and deck plan

Plan 02 Main deck
Battery deck
Middle deck

Plan 03 Lower deck
Platform deck
Lower platform deck and stowing

Plan 04 Superstructure
Bridges

Plan 05 Sectional drawings

Plan 06 Sectional drawing and deck plan according to official set of drawings

Plan 07 Transverse sections IV-X according to official set of drawings

Plan 08 Transverse sections XI-XV according to official set of drawings

Plan 06 Lines and frames

Plan 01

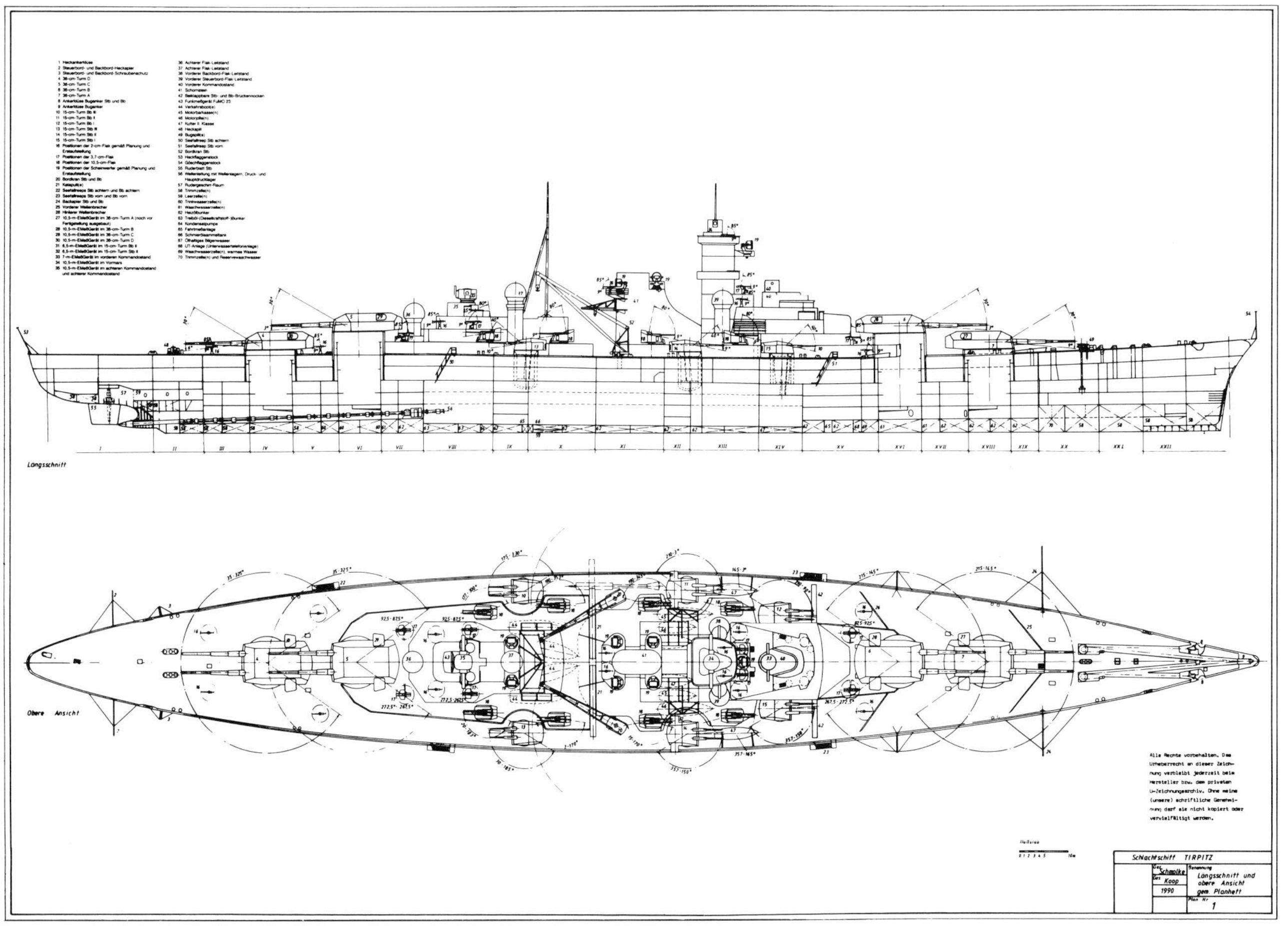

Plan 02

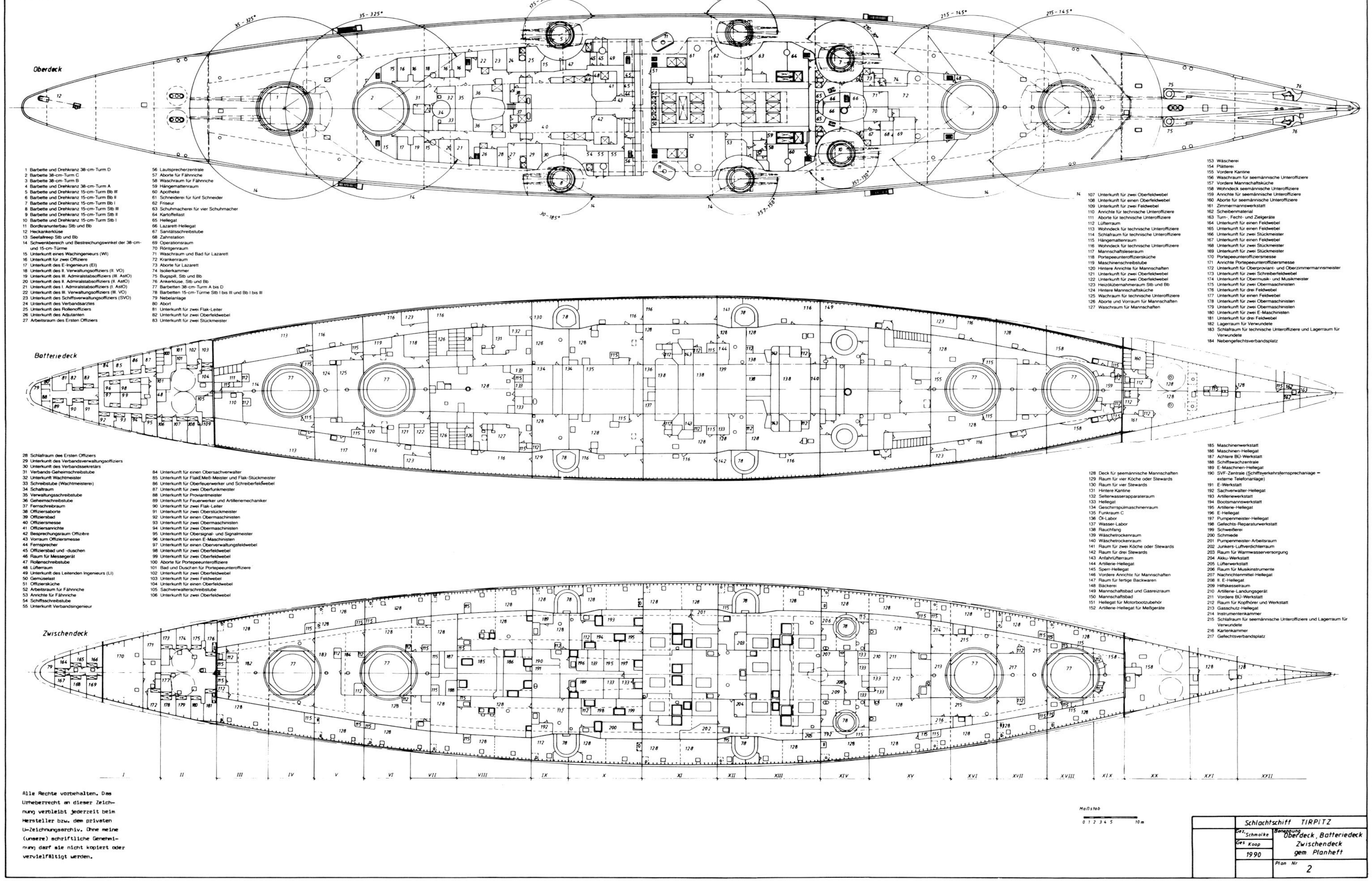

Oberdeck
Batteriedeck
Zwischendeck
1 Barbette und Drehkranz 38-cm-Turm D
2 Barbette 38-cm-Turm C
3 Barbette 38-cm-Turm B
4 Barbette und Drehkranz 38-cm-Turm A
5 Barbette und Drehkranz 15-cm-Turm Bb III
6 Barbette und Drehkranz 15-cm-Turm Bb II
7 Barbette und Drehkranz 15-cm-Turm Bb I
8 Barbette und Drehkranz 15-cm-Turm Stb III
9 Barbette und Drehkranz 15-cm-Turm Stb II
10 Barbette und Drehkranz 15-cm-Turm Stb I
11 Bordkranunterbau Stb und Bb
12 Heckankerklüse
13 Seefallreep Stb und Bb
14 Schwenkbereich und Bestreichungswinkel der 38-cm- und 15-cm-Türme
15 Unterkunft eines Wachingenieurs (WI)
16 Unterkunft für zwei Offiziere
17 Unterkunft des E-Ingenieurs (EI)
18 Unterkunft des II. Verwaltungsoffiziers (II. VO)
19 Unterkunft des III. Admiralstabsoffiziers (III. AstO)
20 Unterkunft des II. Admiralstabsoffiziers (II. AstO)
21 Unterkunft des I. Admiralstabsoffiziers (I. AstO)
22 Unterkunft des III. Verwaltungsoffiziers (III. VO)
23 Unterkunft des Schiffsverwaltungsoffiziers (SVO)
24 Unterkunft des Verbandsarztes
25 Unterkunft des Rollenoffiziers
26 Unterkunft des Adjutanten
27 Arbeitsraum des Ersten Offiziers
28 Schlafraum des Ersten Offiziers
29 Unterkunft des Verbandsverwaltungsoffiziers
30 Unterkunft des Verbandssekretärs
31 Verbands-Geheimschreibstube
32 Unterkunft Wachtmeister
33 Schreibstube (Wachtmeisterei)
34 Schaltraum
35 Verwaltungsschreibstube
36 Geheimschreibstube
37 Fernschreibraum
38 Offiziersaborte
39 Offiziersbad
40 Offiziersmesse
41 Offiziersanrichte
42 Besprechungsraum Offiziere
43 Vorraum Offiziersmesse
44 Fernsprecher
45 Offiziersbad und -duschen
46 Raum für Messegerät
47 Rollenschreibstube
48 Lüfterraum
49 Unterkunft des Leitenden Ingenieurs (LI)
50 Gemüselast
51 Offiziersküche
52 Arbeitsraum für Fähnriche
53 Anrichte für Fähnriche
54 Schiffsschreibstube
55 Unterkunft Verbandsingenieur
56 Lautsprecherzentrale
57 Aborte für Fähnriche
58 Waschraum für Fähnriche
59 Hängemattenraum
60 Apotheke
61 Schneiderei für fünf Schneider
62 Friseur
63 Schuhmacherei für vier Schuhmacher
64 Kartoffellast
65 Hellegat
66 Lazarett-Hellegat
67 Sanitätsschreibstube
68 Zahnstation
69 Operationsraum
70 Röntgenraum
71 Waschraum und Bad für Lazarett
72 Krankenraum
73 Aborte für Lazarett
74 Isolierkammer
75 Bugspill, Stb und Bb
76 Ankerklüse, Stb und Bb
77 Barbetten 38-cm-Turm A bis D
78 Barbetten 15-cm-Türme Stb I bis III und Bb I bis III
79 Nebelanlage
80 Abort
81 Unterkunft für zwei Flak-Leiter
82 Unterkunft für zwei Oberfeldwebel
83 Unterkunft für zwei Stückmeister
84 Unterkunft für einen Obersachverwalter
85 Unterkunft für FlakEMeß-Meister und Flak-Stückmeister
86 Unterkunft für Oberfeuerwerker und Schreiberfeldwebel
87 Unterkunft für zwei Oberfunkmeister
88 Unterkunft für Proviantmeister
89 Unterkunft für Feuerwerker und Artilleriemechaniker
90 Unterkunft für zwei Flak-Leiter
91 Unterkunft für zwei Oberstückmeister
92 Unterkunft für einen Obermaschinisten
93 Unterkunft für zwei Obermaschinisten
94 Unterkunft für zwei Obermaschinisten
95 Unterkunft für Obersignal- und Signalmeister
96 Unterkunft für einen E-Maschinisten
97 Unterkunft für einen Oberverwaltungsfeldwebel
98 Unterkunft für zwei Oberfeldwebel
99 Unterkunft für zwei Oberfeldwebel
100 Aborte für Portepeeunteroffiziere
101 Bad und Duschen für Portepeeunteroffiziere
102 Unterkunft für zwei Oberfeldwebel
103 Unterkunft für zwei Feldwebel
104 Unterkunft für einen Oberfeldwebel
105 Sachverwalterschreibstube
106 Unterkunft für zwei Oberfeldwebel
107 Unterkunft für zwei Oberfeldwebel
108 Unterkunft für einen Oberfeldwebel
109 Unterkunft für zwei Feldwebel
110 Anrichte für technische Unteroffiziere
111 Aborte für technische Unteroffiziere
112 Lüfterraum
113 Wohndeck für technische Unteroffiziere
114 Schlafraum für technische Unteroffiziere
115 Hängemattenraum
116 Wohndeck für technische Unteroffiziere
117 Mannschaftsleseraum
118 Portepeeunteroffiziersküche
119 Maschinenschreibstube
120 Hintere Anrichte für Mannschaften
121 Unterkunft für zwei Oberfeldwebel
122 Unterkunft für zwei Oberfeldwebel
123 Heizölübernahmeraum Stb und Bb
124 Hintere Mannschaftsküche
125 Wachraum für technische Unteroffiziere
126 Aborte und Vorraum für Mannschaften
127 Waschraum für Mannschaften
128 Deck für seemännische Mannschaften
129 Raum für vier Köche oder Stewards
130 Raum für vier Stewards
131 Hintere Kantine
132 Selterwasserapparateraum
133 Hellegat
134 Geschirrspülmaschinenraum
135 Funkraum C
136 Öl-Labor
137 Wasser-Labor
138 Rauchfang
139 Wäschetrockenraum
140 Wäschetrockenraum
141 Raum für zwei Köche oder Stewards
142 Raum für drei Stewards
143 Anfahrlüfterraum
144 Artillerie-Hellegat
145 Sperr-Hellegat
146 Vordere Anrichte für Mannschaften
147 Raum für fertige Backwaren
148 Bäckerei
149 Mannschaftsbad und Gasreizraum
150 Mannschaftsbad
151 Hellegat für Motorbootzubehör
152 Artillerie-Hellegat für Meßgeräte
153 Wäscherei
154 Plätterei
155 Vordere Kantine
156 Waschraum für seemännische Unteroffiziere
157 Vordere Mannschaftsküche
158 Wohndeck seemännische Unteroffiziere
159 Anrichte für seemännische Unteroffiziere
160 Aborte für seemännische Unteroffiziere
161 Zimmermannswerkstatt
162 Scheibenmaterial
163 Turn-, Fecht- und Zielgeräte
164 Unterkunft für einen Feldwebel
165 Unterkunft für einen Feldwebel
166 Unterkunft für zwei Stückmeister
167 Unterkunft für einen Feldwebel
168 Unterkunft für zwei Stückmeister
169 Unterkunft für zwei Stückmeister
170 Portepeeunteroffiziersmesse
171 Anrichte Portepeeunteroffiziersmesse
172 Unterkunft für Oberproviant- und Oberzimmermannsmeister
173 Unterkunft für zwei Schreiberfeldwebel
174 Unterkunft für Obermusik- und Musikmeister
175 Unterkunft für zwei Obermaschinisten
176 Unterkunft für drei Feldwebel
177 Unterkunft für einen Feldwebel
178 Unterkunft für zwei Obermaschinisten
179 Unterkunft für zwei Obermaschinisten
180 Unterkunft für zwei E-Maschinisten
181 Unterkunft für drei Feldwebel
182 Lagerraum für Verwundete
183 Schlafraum für technische Unteroffiziere und Lagerraum für Verwundete
184 Nebengefechtsverbandsplatz
185 Maschinenwerkstatt
186 Maschinen-Hellegat
187 Achtere BÜ-Werkstatt
188 Schiffswachzentrale
189 E-Maschinen-Hellegat
190 SVF-Zentrale (Schiffsverkehrsfernsprechanlage – externe Telefonanlage)
191 E-Werkstatt
192 Sachverwalter-Hellegat
193 Artilleriewerkstatt
194 Bootsmannswerkstatt
195 Artillerie-Hellegat
196 E-Hellegat
197 Pumpenmeister-Hellegat
198 Gefechts-Reparaturwerkstatt
199 Schweißerei
200 Schmiede
201 Pumpenmeister-Arbeitsraum
202 Junkers-Luftverdichterraum
203 Raum für Warmwasserversorgung
204 Akku-Werkstatt
205 Lüfterwerkstatt
206 Raum für Musikinstrumente
207 Nachrichtenmittel-Hellegat
208 II. E-Hellegat
209 Hilfskesselraum
210 Artillerie-Landungsgerät
211 Vordere BÜ-Werkstatt
212 Raum für Kopfhörer und Werkstatt
213 Gasschutz-Hellegat
214 Instrumentenkammer
215 Schlafraum für seemännische Unteroffiziere und Lagerraum für Verwundete
216 Kartenkammer
217 Gefechtsverbandsplatz
Maßstab
0 1 2 3 4 5 10 m
Schlachtschiff TIRPITZ
Gez. Schmolke
Ges Koop
1990
Benennung Oberdeck, Batteriedeck Zwischendeck gem Planheft
Plan Nr 2
Alle Rechte vorbehalten. Das Urheberrecht an dieser Zeichnung verbleibt jederzeit beim Hersteller bzw. dem privaten U-Zeichnungsarchiv. Ohne meine (unsere) schriftliche Genehmigung darf sie nicht kopiert oder vervielfältigt werden.

Plan 03

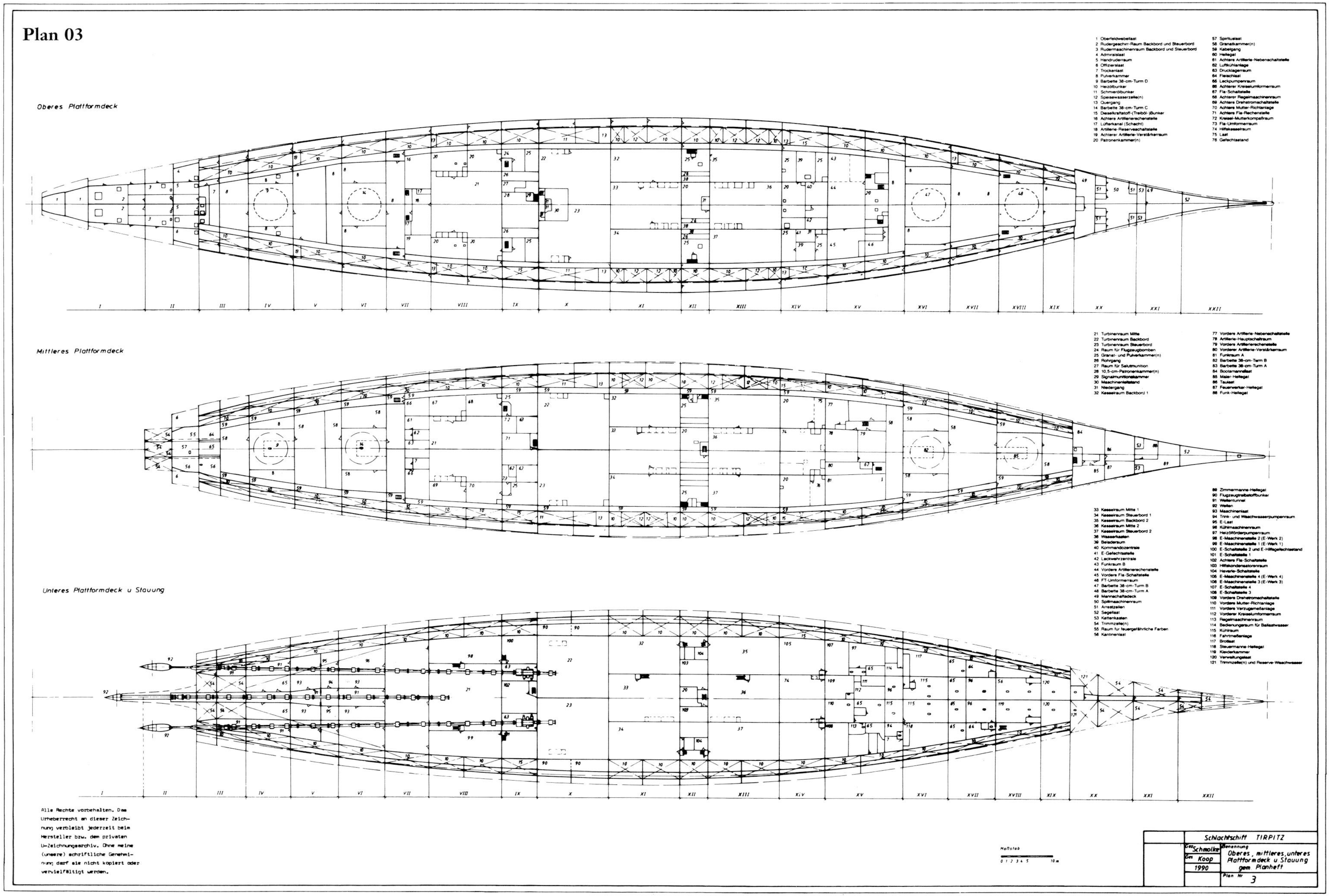

Oberes Plattformdeck
Mittleres Plattformdeck
Unteres Plattformdeck u Stauung
I II III IV V VI VII VIII IX X XI XII XIII XIV XV XVI XVII XVIII XIX XX XXI XXII
1 Oberfeldwebellast
2 Rudergeschirr-Raum Backbord und Steuerbord
3 Rudermaschinenraum Backbord und Steuerbord
4 Admiralslast
5 Handruderraum
6 Offizierslast
7 Trockenlast
8 Pulverkammer
9 Barbette 38-cm-Turm D
10 Heizölbunker
11 Schmierölbunker
12 Speisewasserzelle(n)
13 Quergang
14 Barbette 38-cm-Turm C
15 Dieselkraftstoff-(Treiböl-)Bunker
16 Achtere Artillerierechenstelle
17 Lüfterkanal (Schacht)
18 Artillerie-Reserveschaltstelle
19 Achterer Artillerie-Verstärkerraum
20 Patronenkammer(n)
57 Spirituslast
58 Granatkammer(n)
59 Kabelgang
60 Hellegat
61 Achtere Artillerie-Nebenschaltstelle
62 Luftkühlanlage
63 Drucklagerraum
64 Fleischlast
65 Leckpumpenraum
66 Achterer Kreiselumformerraum
67 Fla-Schaltstelle
68 Achterer Regelmaschinenraum
69 Achtere Drehstromschaltstelle
70 Achtere Mutter-Richtanlage
71 Achtere Fla-Rechenstelle
72 Kreisel-Mutterkompaßraum
73 Fla-Umformerraum
74 Hilfskesselraum
75 Last
76 Gefechtsstand
21 Turbinenraum Mitte
22 Turbinenraum Backbord
23 Turbinenraum Steuerbord
24 Raum für Flugzeugbomben
25 Granat- und Pulverkammer(n)
26 Rohrgang
27 Raum für Salutmunition
28 10,5-cm-Patronenkammer(n)
29 Signalmunitionskammer
30 Maschinenleitstand
31 Niedergang
32 Kesselraum Backbord 1
77 Vordere Artillerie-Nebenschaltstelle
78 Artillerie-Hauptschaltraum
79 Vordere Artillerierechenstelle
80 Vorderer Artillerie-Verstärkerraum
81 Funkraum A
82 Barbette 38-cm-Turm B
83 Barbette 38-cm-Turm A
84 Bootsmannslast
85 Maler-Hellegat
86 Taulast
87 Feuerwerker-Hellegat
88 Funk-Hellegat
33 Kesselraum Mitte 1
34 Kesselraum Steuerbord 1
35 Kesselraum Backbord 2
36 Kesselraum Mitte 2
37 Kesselraum Steuerbord 2
38 Wasserkasten
39 Beladeraum
40 Kommandozentrale
41 E-Gefechtsstelle
42 Leckwehrzentrale
43 Funkraum B
44 Vordere Artillerierechenstelle
45 Vordere Fla-Schaltstelle
46 FT-Umformerraum
47 Barbette 38-cm-Turm B
48 Barbette 38-cm-Turm A
49 Mannschaftsdeck
50 Spillmaschinenraum
51 Arrestzellen
52 Segellast
53 Kettenkasten
54 Trimmzelle(n)
55 Raum fur feuergefährliche Farben
56 Kantinenlast
89 Zimmermanns-Hellegat
90 Flugzeugtreibstoffbunker
91 Wellentunnel
92 Wellen
93 Maschinenlast
94 Trink- und Waschwasserpumpenraum
95 E-Last
96 Kühlmaschinenraum
97 Heizölförderpumpenraum
98 E-Maschinenstelle 2 (E-Werk 2)
99 E-Maschinenstelle 1 (E-Werk 1)
100 E-Schaltstelle 2 und E-Hilfsgefechtsstand
101 E-Schaltstelle 1
102 Achtere Fla-Schaltstelle
103 Hilfskondensatorenraum
104 Havarie-Schaltstelle
105 E-Maschinenstelle 4 (E-Werk 4)
106 E-Maschinenstelle 3 (E-Werk 3)
107 E-Schaltstelle 4
108 E-Schaltstelle 3
109 Vordere Drehstromschaltstelle
110 Vordere Mutter-Richtanlage
111 Vordere Verzugsmeßanlage
112 Vorderer Kreiselumformerraum
113 Regelmaschinenraum
114 Bedienungsraum für Ballastwasser
115 Kühlraum
116 Fahrtmeßanlage
117 Brotlast
118 Steuermanns-Hellegat
119 Kleiderkammer
120 Verwaltungslast
121 Trimmzelle(n) und Reserve-Waschwasser
Alle Rechte vorbehalten. Das Urheberrecht an dieser Zeichnung verbleibt jederzeit beim Hersteller bzw. dem privaten U-Zeichnungsarchiv. Ohne meine (unsere) schriftliche Genehmigung darf sie nicht kopiert oder vervielfältigt werden.
Maßstab
0 1 2 3 4 5 10 m
Schlachtschiff TIRPITZ
Gez. Schmolke
Ges. Koop
1990
Benennung
Oberes, mittleres, unteres Plattformdeck u Stauung gem Planheft
Plan Nr 3

1 Arbeitsraum Meteorologe
2 Bildfunk-Raum
3 Schutzstand
4 Kartenhaus
5 Nachrichtenzentrale
6 Admiralsbrückenkammer
7 Abort
8 Unterkunft für einen Oberfeldwebel
9 Unterkunft für zwei Oberfeldwebel
10 Unterkunft für zwei Feldwebel
11 Unterkunft für zwei Oberfeldwebel
12 Unterkunft für Sanitätsoberfeldwebel
13 Dunkelkammer
14 Abort Portepeeunteroffiziere
15 Abort Offiziere
16 Unterkunft für Reichkriegsgerichtsrat
17 Unterkunft für I. ATO (Erster Artillerie-Technischer Offizier)
18 Unterkunft für II. ATO (Zweiter Artillerie-Technischer Offizier)
19 Unterkunft für zwei Offiziere
20 Unterkunft für I. NO (Erster Navigationsoffizier)
21 Unterkunft für Funkoffizier
22 Unterkunft für I. Hilfsarzt
23 Unterkunft für zwei Offiziere
24 Horchstelle
25 Lüfterumformerraum
26 UK-Stelle (Raum für Ultrakurzwelle)
27 Unterkunft für zwei Offiziere
28 Unterkunft für Wachoffiziere
29 Schaltraum
30 Schutzraum für Munitionsmanner
31 Offiziersdusche
32 Offiziersbad
33 Lüfterraum
34 Übungsraum
35 Hellegat
36 Raum für 10,5-m-Basisgerät
37 Artillerieschreibstube
38 Unterkunft I. AO (Erster Artillerieoffizier)
39 Unterkunft II. AO (Zweiter Artillerieoffizier)
40 Unterkunft für weitere Artillerieoffiziere
41 Unterkunft Schiffsarzt
42 Unterkunft Schiffsarzt (Kriegszuschlag)
43 Kommandobrücke
44 Schutzstand Schiffsführung
45 Schiffskartenhaus
46 Schutzstand Nachtleitstand
47 Kommandobrückenkammer
48 Unterkunft für zwei Offiziere
49 Unterkunft für zwei Leutnante
50 Unterkunft für zwei Leutnante
51 Unterkunft für zwei Leutnante
52 Unterkunft für zwei Leutnante
53 Unterkunft für zwei Leutnante
54 Unterkunft für zwei Leutnante
55 Unterkunft für zwei Offiziere
56 Unterkunft für zwei Offiziere
57 Unterkunft für zwei Offiziere
58 Unterkunft für zwei Offiziere
59 Unterkunft für einen Artillerieoffizier (Kriegszuschlag)

Hinweis: Bei einigen der diesem Plan zugehörigen Rissen fehlt in den Originalunterlagen jegliche Beschriftung. Daher wurde hier ebenfalls auf eine Numerierung verzichtet; sie wäre rein spekulativ.
Für alle anderen Pläne gilt gleiches: auch hier wurde bei den unzähligen Durchbrüchen in den Schotts, bei den vielen Niedergängen, Mannlöchern, Schotten (Türen) und sonstigen Markierungen darauf verzichtet.

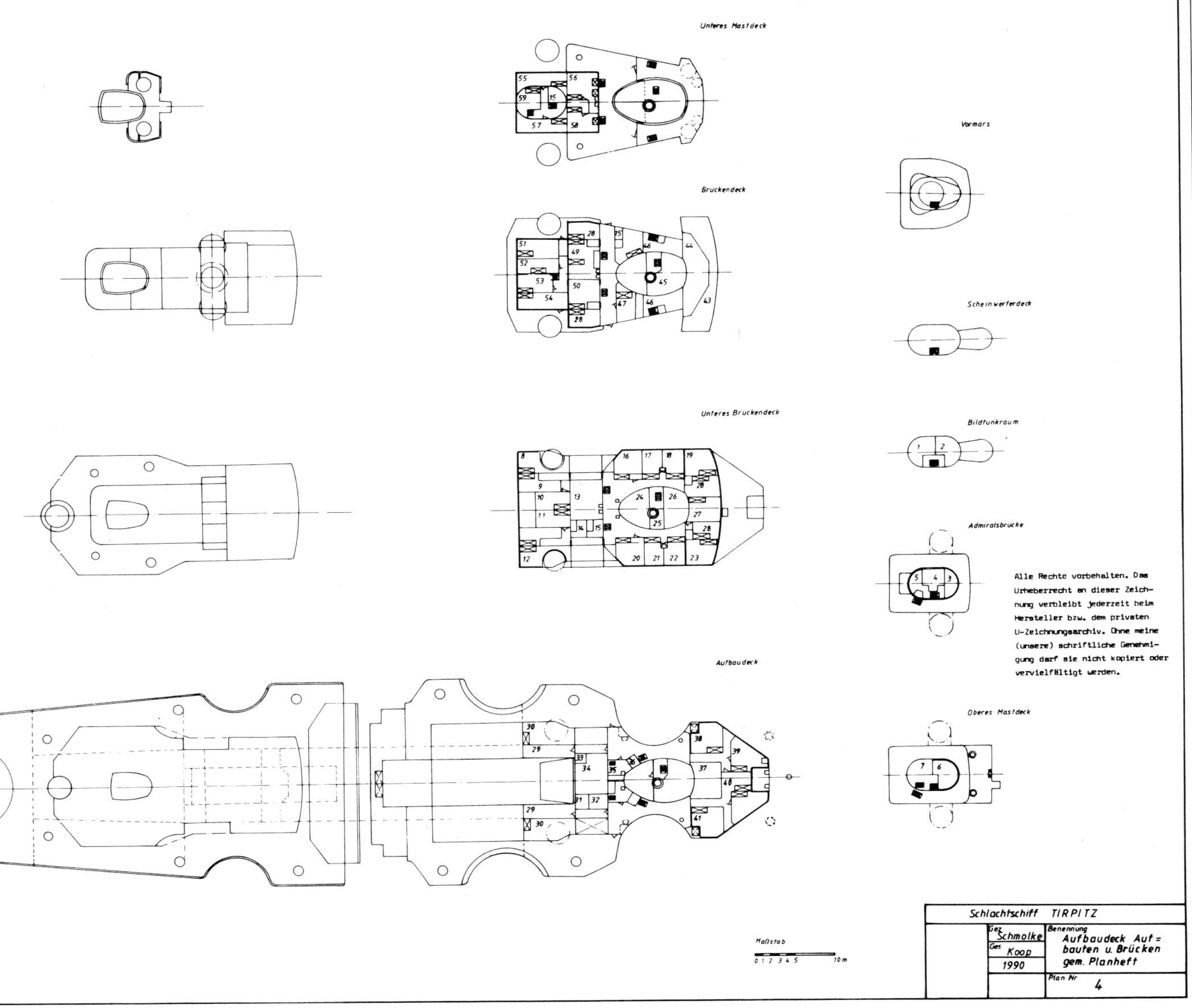

Plan 04

Plan 05

1 Unterkunft für zwei Oberstückmeister
2 Unterkunft Waffenleitvormann achtern und Reserve-Flak-Leiter
3 Unterkunft für einen Feldwebel
4 Unterkunft für zwei Stückmeister
5 Reserve-Kleiderkammer
6 Trimmzelle
7 Raum Obersachverwalter
8 Unterkunft E-Maschinist(en)
9 Unterkunft Oberverwaltungsfeldwebel
10 Unterkunft Obermaschinist(en)
11 Portepeeunteroffiziersmesse
12 Rudergeschirr-Raum
13 Mittelschraube
14 Backbordruder
15 Steuerbordruder
16 Schraubenschutz Backbord
17 Schraubenschutz Steuerbord
18 Unterkunft für zwei Oberfunkmeister
19 Unterkunft Obersignalmeister/Signalmeister
20 Anrichte Portepeeunteroffiziersmesse
21 Lüfterraum
22 Raum Oberproviantmeister/Oberzimmermeister
23 Rudergeschirr-Raum
24 Leerzelle
25 Backbordschraube
26 Steuerbordschraube
27 Poller
28 Heckspill Backbord und Steuerbord
29 Bade- und Duschräume
30 Unterkunft für zwei Oberfeldwebel
31 Unterkunft für Obermusikmeister/Musikmeister
32 Unterkunft für zwei Obermaschinisten
33 Rudermaschinenraum Backbord und Steuerbord
34 Trimmzelle
35 Backbord-Wellenbock
36 Steuerbord-Wellenbock
37 Unterkunft für zwei Feldwebel
38 Unterkunft für Oberfeldwebel
39 Schreibstube Sachverwalter
40 Unterkunft für drei Feldwebel
41 Admiralslast
42 Offizierslast
43 Handruderraum Backbord
44 Handruderraum Steuerbord
45 Spirituslast
46 Raum für feuergefährliche Farben
47 Kantinenlast
48 Wellentunnel Mittelwelle
49 Trimmzelle
50 Wellenbock Backbord und Steuerbord
51 Wohndeck technische Unteroffiziere
52 Schlafraum technische Unteroffiziere
53 Deck seemännische Mannschaften
54 Lagerraum für Verwundete
55 Pulverkammer
56 Granatkammer
57 Kabelführungsbahnen
58 Wellentunnel Backbordwelle
59 Wellentunnel Steuerbordwelle
60 Wellentunnel Mittelwelle
61 Trimmzelle
62 Trimmzelle
63 Heizölbunker
64 38-cm-Turm
65 Trimm- und Reservewaschwasserzelle
66 Beladeraum
67 Pulverkammer
68 Deck technische Mannschaften
69 Deck seemännische Mannschaften
70 Waschraum technische Unteroffiziere
71 Mannschaftsleseraum
72 Schlafraum technische Mannschaften und Lagerraum für Verwundete
73 Nebengefechtsverbandsplatz
74 Pulverkammer
75 Granatkammer
76 Maschinenlast
77 Wellentunnel Backbordwelle
78 Wellentunnel Mittelwelle
79 Wellentunnel Steuerbordwelle
80 Leerzelle
81 Niedergang
82 38-cm-Turm C
83 Maschinenschreibstube
84 Hintere Anrichte für Mannschaften
85 Kühlmaschinenraum
86 Heizölförderpumpenraum
87 Waschwasserzelle
88 achterer Flakleitstand
89 Unterkunft II. Verwaltungsoffizier (II. VO)
90 Unterkunft Wachingenieur
91 Mannschaftsaborte
92 achtere BÜ-Werkstatt
93 Schiffs-Wachzentrale
94 E-Last
95 achtere Artillerie-Rechenstelle
96 Lüfterschacht/-kanal
97 Reserve-Artillerieschaltstelle
98 achterer Artillerie-Verstärkerraum
99 Hellegat
100 achtere Artillerie-Nebenschaltstelle
101 Luftkühlanlage
102 Drucklagerraum Mitte
103 Trockenlast
104 achterer Kreiselumformerraum
105 Kommandantenlast
106 Feuerwerker-Hellegat
107 E-Maschinenstelle (WE - E-Werk 1)
108 achterer Kommandostand mit 10,5-m-Basisgerät
109 Quergang
110 Hängemattenraum
111 Verwaltungsschreibstube
112 Maschinenwerkstatt
113 Turbinenraum Mitte
114 E-Maschinenstelle 2 (E-Werk 2)
115 E-Maschinenstelle 1 (E-Werk 1)
116 Patronenkammer
117 Havarie-Schaltstelle
118 achtere Drehstromschaltstelle
119 Speisewasserzelle
120 Zelle für ölhaltiges Bilgenwasser
121 Schmierölsammeltank
122 Leerzelle
123 Unterkunft Verbandsarzt
124 Offiziersaborte
125 Fernschreibstelle
126 Offiziersbad
127 Arbeitsraum Erster Offizier (IO)
128 Raum für Selterswasserapparat
129 Hellegat
130 Maschinen-Hellegat
131 Bierlast
132 achterer Regelmaschinenraum
133 achtere Mutterrichtanlage
134 Überlaufzelle
135 Kondensatzelle
136 Kondensatpumpenraum
137 Großmast
138 Beiboote
139 15-cm-Türme Backbord III und Steuerbord III
140 Lüfterraum
141 Offiziersmesse
142 Geschirrspülmaschinenraum
143 Dieselkraftstoffbunker (Treiböl)
144 Rohrgang
145 Granat- und Pulverkammer
146 10,5-cm-Patronenkammer
147 achtere Flak-Rechenstelle
148 achtere Flak-Schaltstelle
149 Gang
150 Fahrtmeßanlage
151 Unterkunft Leitender Ingenieur (LI)
152 Anrichte Offiziersmesse
153 Vorraum Offiziersmesse
154 Besprechungsraum
155 Unterkunft Verbands-Ingenieur
156 Turbinenraum Backbord
157 Turbinenraum Steuerbord
158 Schmieröltank
159 Flugzeugtreibstoff
160 Luftmelderaum
161 Maschinenlast
162 Funkraum C
163 Artillerie-Werkstatt
164 Bootsmannswerkstatt
165 Artillerie-Hellegat
166 Artillerie-Reparaturwerkstatt
167 Schmiede
168 Hangar
169 Schweißerei
170 Pumpenmeister-Hellegat
171 Quergang
172 Kran Backbord
173 Kran Steuerbord
174 2-cm-Flak Backbord-Schornsteinplattform
175 2-cm-Flak Steuerbord-Schornsteinplattform
176 Flak-Leitgerät Backbord und Steuerbord-Schornsteinplattform
177 Drehkran Backbord und Steuerbord, Schornsteinmantel
178 Offiziersküche
179 Lüfterraum
180 Kesselraum Backbord 1
181 Kesselraum Mitte 1
182 Kesselraum Steuerbord 1
183 Schornsteinmantel
184 Scheinwerfer Backbord Schornsteinplattform
185 Scheinwerfer Steuerbord Schornsteinplattform
186 Arbeitsraum für Fähnriche
187 Schneiderei
188 Friseur
189 Pumpenmeisterei
190 Junkers-Luftverdichterraum
191 15-cm-Turm Backbord I
192 15-cm-Turm Steuerbord I
193 Schutzstand
194 Kartenhaus
195 Unterkunft II. Artillerieoffizier (II. AO)
196 Unterkunft Funkoffizier
197 Lüfter- und Umformerraum
198 Lazarett-Hellegat
199 Mannschaftsbad und Gasreizraum
200 Mannschaftsbad
201 Beladeraum
202 Kabelführungsbahn
203 Hellegat II E und Nachrichtenmittel-Hellegat
204 E-Gefechtsstelle
205 Hilfskesselraum
206 E-Maschinenstelle 4 (E-Werk 4)
207 E-Maschinenstelle 3 (E-Werk 3)
208 Unterkunft I. Artillerieoffizier (I. AO)
209 Unterkunft Schiffsarzt
210 Isolierkammer
211 Krankenraum
212 Operationsraum
213 Mannschaftsaborte
214 Seefallreep
215 vordere BÜ-Werkstatt
216 Raum für Kopfhörer und Werkstatt
217 Taulast
218 Funkraum B
219 vordere Artillerie-Rechenstelle
220 vordere Artillerie-Schaltstelle
221 Umformerraum für FT (Funkanlagen)
222 Funkraum A
223 38-cm-Turm B
224 Schlafraum seemännische Unteroffiziere und Lagerraum Verwaltung
225 Brotlast
226 Steuermanns-Hellegat
227 Kühlraum
228 Trinkwasserzelle
229 Heizölförderpumpenraum
230 vorderer Kreiselumformerraum
231 Luftkühlanlage
232 Artillerieverstärkerraum
233 Regelmaschinenraum
234 Wohndeck seemännische Unteroffiziere
235 Gefechtsverbandsplatz
236 Leckpumpenraum XVII.2
237 Leckpumpenraum XVII.1
238 38-cm-Turm A
239 Wohndeck seemännische Unteroffiziere
240 Kantinenlast
241 Kleiderkammer
242 Lüfterraum
243 Anrichte für seemännische Unteroffiziere
244 Sachverwalterlast
245 Bugspill Backbord und Steuerbord
246 Spillmaschinenraum
247 Feuerwerker-Hellegat
248 Rohrgang
249 Kettenkasten Backbord und Steuerbord
250 Funk-Hellegat II E
251 Poller
252 Mannschaftsraum
253 Zimmermanns-Hellegat
254 Segellast
255 Arbeitsraum des Meteorologen
256 Nachrichtenzentrale
257 Aborte
258 Unterkunft für zwei Offiziere
259 Unterkunft für Artillerieoffizier
260 Unterkunft für zwei Leutnante
261 Unterkunft für einen Leutnant
262 Unterkunft für einen Oberfeldwebel
263 Unterkunft für zwei Oberfeldwebel
264 Unterkunft für Sanitätsoberfeldwebel
265 Raum für Munitionsmänner
266 Schaltraum
267 Raum für vier Schuhmacher
268 Förderwerk
269 Aborte für Fähnriche
270 Überlaufzellen
271 Kesselraum Backbord 2
272 Kesselraum Mitte 2
273 Kesselraum Steuerbord 2
274 Vormarsstand mit 10,5-m-Basisgerät
275 Unterkunft für Wachoffizier
276 Dunkelkammer
277 Aborte für Portepee-Unteroffiziere
278 Hör-Übungsraum
279 Kartoffellast
280 Apotheke

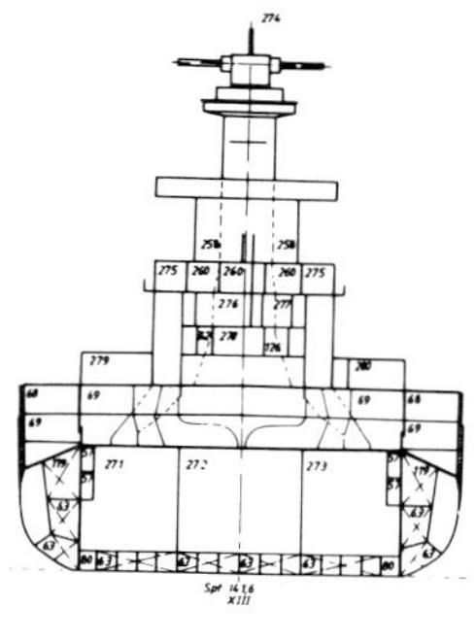

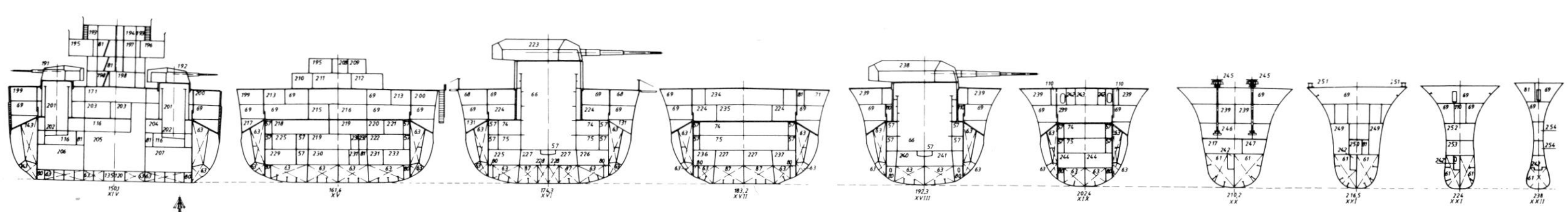

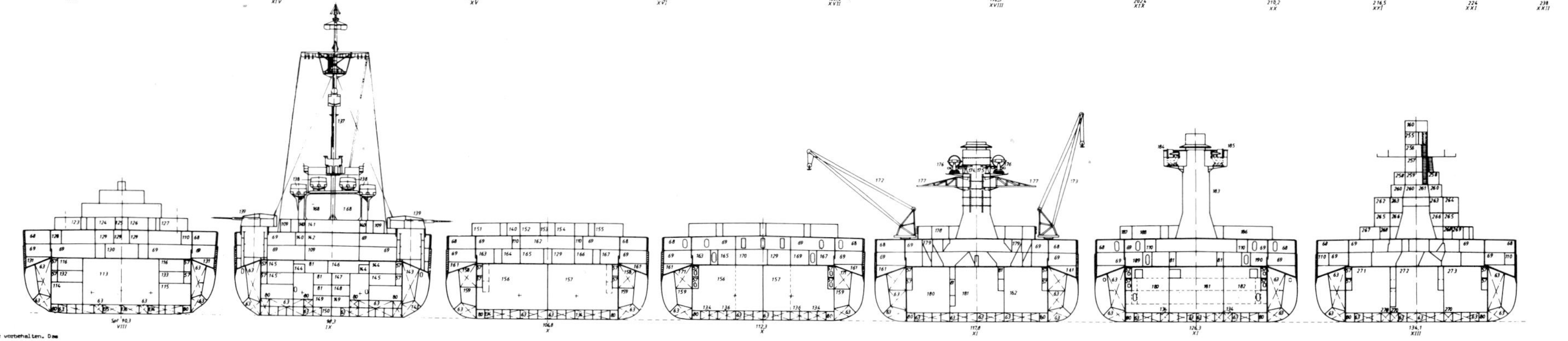

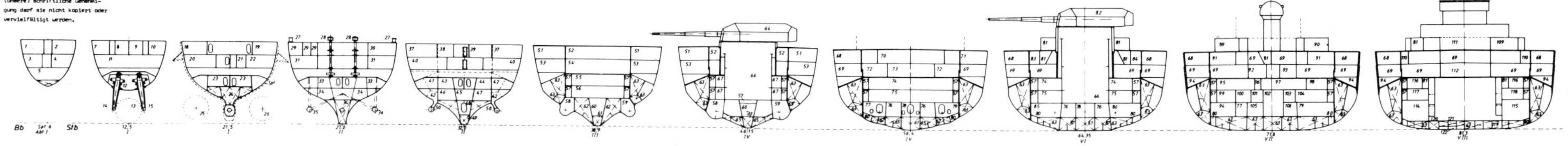

Maßstab 0 1 2 3 4 5 10m

	Schlachtschiff TIRPITZ
Maßstab	Gez. Schmolke; Ges Koop; 1990 — Benennung: Querschnitte nach Planheft
	Plan-Nr 5

Plan 06

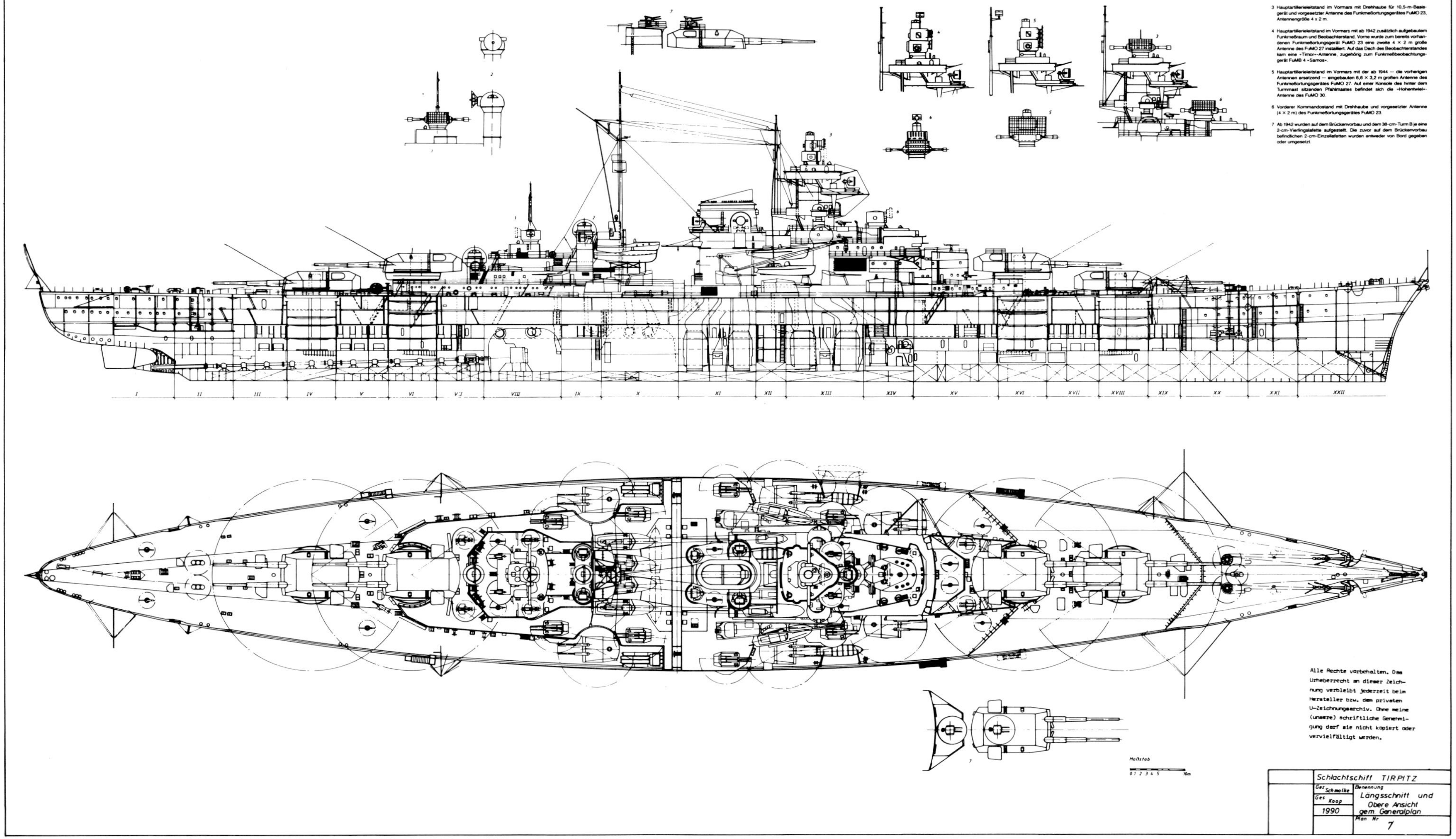

1 Achterer Kommandostand mit Drehhaube und 10,5-m-Basisgerät sowie Funkmeßortungsgerät FuMO 23, Antennengröße 4 × 2 m.

2 Achterer Flakleitstand mit vorgesetztem Funkmeßortungsgerät FuMO 213 »Würzburg«, Antennendurchmesser 3 m. Zum Einbau ab 1944 wurde der Unterbau des Leitstandes um 2 m erhöht.

3 Hauptartillerieleitstand im Vormars mit Drehhaube für 10,5-m-Basisgerät und vorgesetzter Antenne des Funkmeßortungsgerätes FuMO 23, Antennengröße 4 x 2 m.

4 Hauptartillerieleitstand im Vormars mit ab 1942 zusätzlich aufgebautem Funkmeßraum und Beobachterstand. Vorne wurde zum bereits vorhandenen Funkmeßortungsgerät FuMO 23 eine zweite 4 × 2 m große Antenne des FuMO 27 installiert. Auf das Dach des Beobachterstandes kam eine »Timor«-Antenne, zugehörig zum Funkmeßbeobachtungsgerät FuMB 4 »Samos«.

5 Hauptartillerieleitstand im Vormars mit der ab 1944 — die vorherigen Antennen ersetzend — eingebauten 6,6 × 3,2 m großen Antenne des Funkmeßortungsgerätes FuMO 27. Auf einer Konsole des hinter dem Turmmast sitzenden Pfahlmastes befindet sich die »Hohentwiel«-Antenne des FuMO 30.

6 Vorderer Kommandostand mit Drehhaube und vorgesetzter Antenne (4 × 2 m) des Funkmeßortungsgerätes FuMO 23.

7 Ab 1942 wurden auf dem Brückenvorbau und dem 38-cm-Turm B je eine 2-cm-Vierlingslafette aufgestellt. Die zuvor auf dem Brückenvorbau befindlichen 2-cm-Einzellafetten wurden entweder von Bord gegeben oder umgesetzt.

Plan 07

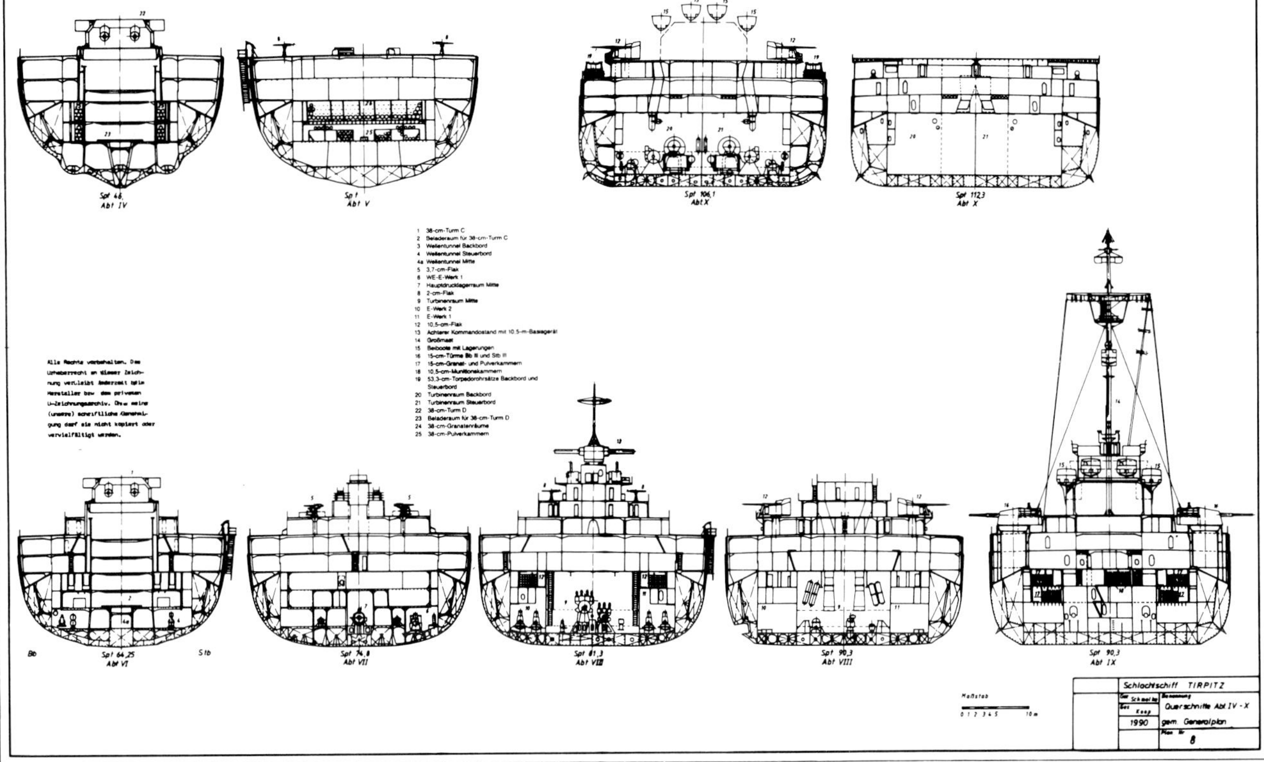

Plan 08

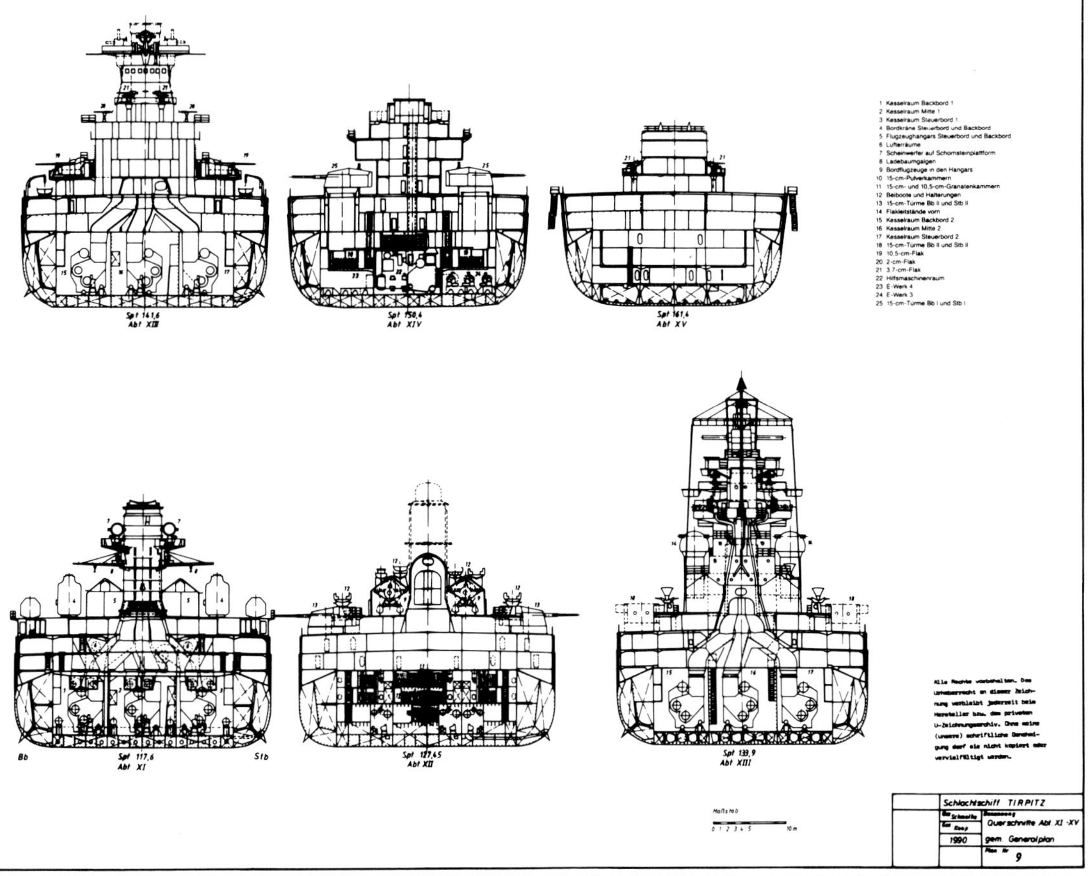

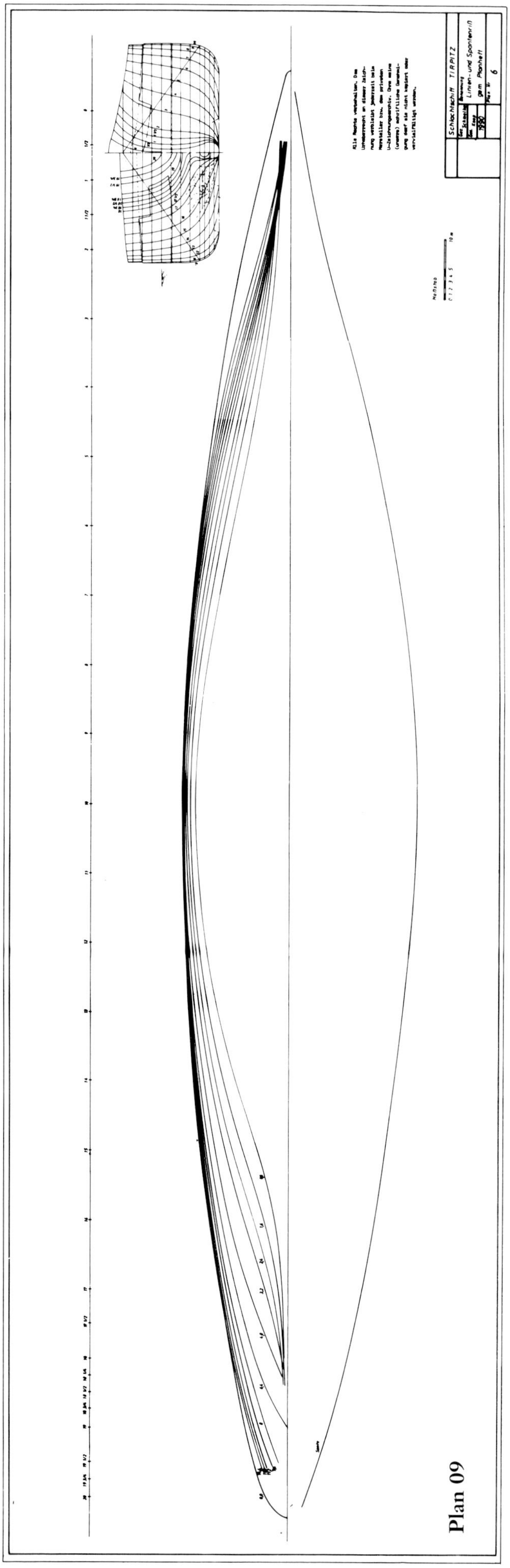

Bibliography

Aßmann, Kurt, *Deutsche Seestrategie in zwei Weltkriegen* (Heidelberg, 1957)
Bennett, Geoffrey, *Seeschlachten im 2. Weltkrieg* (Koblenz/Bonn, 1981)
Brennecke, Jochen, *Schlachtschiff Tirpitz* (Herford, 1978)
Breyer, Siegfried, *Schlachtschiffe und Schlachtkreuzer 1905-1970* (München, 1970)
Breyer, Siegfried, *Großkampfschiffe 1905-1970, Vol 1: Großbritannien und Deutschland* (München, 1977)
Breyer, Siegfried/Koop, Gerhard, *Von der Emden zur Tirpitz*, Vol 1, 2nd print (München, 1982)
Brown, David, *Die Tirpitz* (München, 1980)
Conway's All the World's Fighting Ships 1922-1946 (London, 1980)
Dulin/Garzke, *Battleships*, Vol 3 (Annapolis, 1986)
Evers, *Kriegsschiffbau* (Berlin, 1943)
Friedman, Norman, *Battleships* (London, 1978)
Gröner, Erich, *Die deutschen Kriegsschiffe 1815-1945*, Vol 1, 2nd print (Koblenz, 1989)
Hildebrand, Hans H/Stöhr, Albert/Steinmetz, Hans-Otto, *Die deutschen Kriegsschiffe*, Biographies, Vol 6 (Herford, 1982)
Koop, Gerhard/Schmolke, Klaus-Peter, *Die Schlachtschiffe der Bismarck-Klasse* (Koblenz, 1990)
Koop, Gerhard/Schmolke, Klaus-Peter, *'Planrolle: Schlachtschiff Tirpitz'* (Koblenz, 1990)
Lewin, Ronald, *Entschied ULTRA den Krieg? Allierte Funk-aufklärung im 2. Weltkrieg* (Koblenz/Bonn, 1981)
Lohmann, Walter/Hildebrand, Hans H, *Die deutsche Kriegs-marine 1939-1945: Gliederung, Organisation, Stellenbeset-zung*, 3 vols (Bad Nauheim, 1956-1964)
Peillard, Alistair, *Versenkt die Tirpitz!* (Wiesbaden, 1977)
Pemsel, Helmut, *Seeherrschaft. Eine maritime Weltgeschichte von den Anfängen der Seefahrt bis zur Gegenwart*, 2 vols (Koblenz, 1985)
Potter, Elmer B/Nimitz, Chester W/Rohwer, Jürgen, *Seemacht: Eine Seekriegsgeschichte von der Antike bis zur Gegenwart* (München, 1974)
Raeder, Erich, *Mein Leben*, 2 vols (Tübingen, 1956/57)
Rohwer, Jürgen/Hümmelchen, Gerhard, *Chronik des Seekrieges 1939-1945* (Oldenburg/Hamburg, 1968)
Salewski, Michael, *Die deutsche Seekriegsleitung 1935-1945*,
3 vols (Frankfurt a.M./München, 1970-1975)
Wagner, Gerhard (ed), *Lagevorträge des Oberbefehlshabers der Kriegsmarine vor Hitler 1939-1945* (München, 1972)

Periodicals
Jahrbuch der Schiffbautechnischen Gesellschaft
Marinearsenal
Marineforum
Marine-Rundschau
Schiffbau

Sources
Bundesarchiv/Militärarchiv, Freiburg i Br (drawings)
Motorenwerke Mannheim, Betriebsvorschrift Dieselmotor RS 38 S
Author's archives/Koop

Illustration acknowledgements

Schmolke (3)
Kriegsmarinewerft Wilhelmshaven (8)
PK und Sammlung Koop/Gally (32)
Stadtarchiv Wihelmshaven (1)
Wagner (1)
Hasse (4)
Motorenwerke Mannheim (1)
Drawings and sketches by Klaus-Peter Schmolke

Plan Keys

Note: On some of the original plans all captions are missing. As it would be highly speculative to create new captions, all these have been omitted. We have also not included the many hatches, manholes and companion hatches in our drawings.

PLAN 01

1 hawse, stern anchor
2 booms, starboard and port
3 propeller protectors, starboard and port
4 38cm turret D
5 38cm turret C
6 38cm turret B
7 38cm turret A
8 hawse bow anchors, starboard and port
9 hawse bow anchor
10 15cm turret port III
11 15cm turret port II
12 15cm turret port I
13 15cm turret starboard III
14 15cm turret starboard II
15 15cm turret starboard I
16 position of 2cm AA guns according to plans and initial installation
17 position of 3.7cm AA guns
18 position of 10.5cm AA guns
19 planned position of searchlights
20 crane, starboard and port
21 catapults
22 aft gangways, starboard and port
23 fore gangways, starboard and port
24 boom, starboard and port
25 fore breakwater
26 aft breakwater
27 10.5-m-base rangefinder in 38cm turret A (removed before completion)
28 10.5m base rangefinder in 38cm turret B
29 10.5m base rangefinder in 38cm turret C
30 10.5m base rangefinder in 38cm turret D
31 6.5m base rangefinder in 15cm turret port II
32 6.5m base rangefinder in 15cm turret starboard II
33 7m base rangefinder on fore conning tower
34 10.5m base rangefinder on foretop
35 10.5m base rangefinder on aft conning tower and aft conning tower
36 aft AA director control tower
37 aft AA director control tower
38 fore AA director control tower, port
39 fore AA director control tower, starboard
40 fore conning tower
41 funnel
42 bridge wings, foldable
43 radar set FuMO 32
44 traffic boats
45 motor launch
46 motor pinnace
47 cutter 3. class
48 capstan, stern
49 capstan, bow
50 stern gangway, starboard
51 gangway, starboard
52 crane, starboard
53 stern flag staff
54 jack staff
55 rudder, starboard
56 shafts with bearings
57 steering gear room
58 trim tanks
59 reserve tanks
60 fresh water tank
61 washing water tank
62 oil fuel tank
63 diesel tank
64 evaporation pump
65 speedometer
66 lubrication oil tank
67 oil-polluted bilge water
68 UT-installation
69 washing water tanks, warm water
70 trim tanks and reserve washing water

PLAN 02

1 barbette and training rack 38cm turret D
2 barbette 38cm turret C
3 barbette 38cm turret B
4 barbette and training rack 38cm turret A
5 barbette and training rack 15cm turret port III
6 barbette and training rack 15cm turret port II
7 barbette and training rack 15cm turret port I
8 barbette and training rack 15cm turret starboard III
9 barbette and training rack 15cm turret starboard II
10 barbette and training rack 15cm turret starboard I
11 crane mountings, starboard and port
12 hawse, stern anchor
13 gangways, starboard and port
14 training arcs, 38cm and 15cm turrets
15 cabin for 1 engineer officer (WI)
16 cabin for 2 officers
17 cabin for electrical engineer officer (EI)
18 cabin for admin officer (II.VO)
19 cabin for admiral staff officer (III.AstO)
20 cabin for admiral staff officer (II.AstO)
21 cabin for admiral staff officer (I.AstO)
22 cabin for admin officer (III.VO)
23 cabin for chief admin officer
24 cabin for fleet surgeon
25 cabin for station officer
26 cabin for adjutant
27 executive officer's office
28 executive officer's cabin
29 cabin for fleet admin officer
30 cabin for fleet secretary
31 fleet crypto office
32 provost officer's cabin
33 provost officer's office
34 switchboard room
35 admin office
36 crypto office
37 teleprinters
38 officer's WC
39 officer's bathroom
40 wardroom
41 wardroom pantry
42 officer's conference room
43 ante-room
44 telephones
45 officer's bathroom and showers
46 wardroom store room
47 station officer's office
48 ventilation room
49 cabin for chief engineer officer (LI)
50 vegetable store
51 officer's galley
52 ensign's workroom
53 ensign's pantry
54 chief clerk's office
55 fleet engineer's cabin
56 loudspeaker control room
57 ensign's WC
58 ensign's washroom
59 hammock store
60 pharmacy
61 tailor's shop, for 5 tailors
62 barber
63 shoemaker's shop, for 5 shoemakers
64 potato store
65 store room
66 hospital store room
67 hospital admin office
68 dentist
69 operation theatre
70 X-ray room
71 washroom and bathroom for hospital sickbay
72 sickbay
73 hospital WC
74 isolation ward
75 capstans, bow, starboard and port
76 hawses, starboard and port
77 barbettes 38cm turrets A – D
78 barbettes 15cm turrets starboard I – III and port I – III
79 fog generator
80 WC
81 cabin for 2 AA fire control SNCOs
82 cabin for 2 SNCOs
83 cabin for 2 artillery SNCOs
84 cabin for 1 admin SNCO
85 cabin for AA director control SNCO and AA artillery SNCO
86 cabin for pyrotechnics SNCO and AA artillery SNCO
78 cabin for 2 signals SNCOs
88 cabin for catering SNCO
89 cabin for fireworker and artillery mechanic
90 cabin for 2 AA fire control SNCOs
91 cabin for 2 artillery SNCOs
92 cabin for 1 engineer SNCO
93 cabin for 2 engineer SNCO
94 cabin for 2 engineer SNCO
95 cabin for 1 chief signals SNCO and 1 signals SNCO
96 cabin for electrical engineer SNCO
97 cabin for 1 chief admin SNCO
98 cabin for 2 SNCOs
99 cabin for 2 SNCOs
100 SNCO's WC
101 bathroom and showers for SNCOs
102 cabin for 2 SNCOs
103 cabin for 2 SNCOs
104 cabin for 1 SNCO
105 admin office
106 cabin for 2 SNCOs
107 cabin for 2 SNCOs
108 cabin for 1 SNCO
109 cabin for 2 SNCOs
110 engineer SNCO's pantry
111 engineer SNCO's WC
112 ventilation room
113 engineer NCO's deck
114 engineer SNCO's bedroom
115 hammock store
116 engineer NCO's deck
117 seamen's reading room
118 SNCO's galley
119 engineer section office
120 rear pantry for seamen
121 cabin for 2 SNCOs
122 cabin for 2 SNCOs
123 oil fuel bunker control station starboard and port
124 seamen's galley (rear)
125 watchroom for engineer NCOs
126 seamen's heads
127 seamen's washplace
128 seamen's deck
129 cabin for 4 cooks or stewards
130 cabin for 4 stewards
131 rear canteen
132 mineral water fountain
133 store room
134 dishwashers
135 radio room C
136 oil laboratory
137 water laboratory
138 chimney
139 drying room
140 drying room
141 cabin for 2 cooks or stewards
142 cabin for 3 stewards
143 ventilation room
144 artillery store room
145 boom defence store room
146 seamen's pantry
147 store room for bakery products
148 bakery
149 seamen's bathroom and gas heating
150 seamen's bathroom
151 motor boat accessories store room
152 store room for optical artillery instruments
153 laundry
154 steam laundry
155 canteen
156 NCO's washroom
157 seamen's galley
158 NCO's deck
159 NCO's pantry
160 NCO's WC
161 carpenter's shop
162 target store
163 sports equipment
164 cabin for 1 SNCO
165 cabin for 1 SNCO
166 cabin for 2 artillery SNCOs
167 cabin for 1 SNCO
168 cabin for 2 artillery SNCOs
169 cabin for 2 artillery SNCOs
170 SNCO's mess
171 mess pantry
172 cabin for catering SNCO and carpenter SNCO
173 cabin for 2 clerks
174 cabin for 2 bandleaders
175 cabin for 2 engineer SNCOs
176 cabin for 3 SNCOs
177 cabin for 1 SNCO
178 cabin for 2 engineer SNCOs
179 cabin for 2 engineer SNCOs
180 cabin for 2 electrical engineer SNCOs
181 cabin for 3 SNCO
182 sickbay
183 NCO's deck
184 reserve dressing station
185 engineer workshop
186 workshop store room
187 BÜ-workshop
188 central control station
189 electrical engineering workshop store room
190 telephone switchboard
191 electrical engineering workshop
192 admin office store room
193 artillery workshop
194 bosun's workshop
195 artillery store room
196 electrical engineering workshop store room
197 pumpmaster store room
198 combat repairs workshop
199 welding shop
200 forge
201 pumpmaster's workshop
202 Junkers-compressor room
203 hot water supply room
204 battery workshop
205 ventilator workshop
206 musical instruments store
207 signalling equipment store
208 electrical engineering workshop store room No 2
209 auxiliary boiler room
210 landing party artillery equipment
211 BU-workshop
212 radio workshop
213 gas protection store
214 store room for instruments
215 NCO's sleeping room and reserve hospital
216 chart room
217 combat dressing station

PLAN 03

1 SNCO's store room
2 rudder gear room, starboard and port
3 rudder compartment, starboard and port
4 admiral's store room
5 manual steering room
6 officer's store room
7 dry store
8 powder magazine
9 barbette 38cm turret
10 oil fuel tank
11 lubrication oil tank
12 feed tanks
13 walkway
14 barbette 38cm turret
15 diesel tank
16 aft artillery plotting office
17 ventilation air duct
18 artillery reserve switchboard room
19 aft artillery amplification room
20 cartridge magazines
21 central turbine room
22 turbine room, port
23 turbine room, starboard
24 bomb store
25 shell and powder magazine
26 trunk
27 blank ammunition store
28 10.5cm magazine
29 signalling ammunition store
30 machinery control centre
31 companion hatch
32 boiler room, port 1
33 boiler room, inner 1
34 boiler room, starboard 1
35 boiler room, port 2
36 boiler room, inner 2
37 boiler room, starboard 2
38 water tank
39 store room
40 control station
41 electrical machinery control station
42 damage control centre
43 radio room B
44 fore artillery plotting office
45 fore AA-switchboard room
46 transformer room
47 barbette 38cm turret B
48 barbette 38cm turret A
49 seamen's deck
50 capstan engine room
51 detention cells
52 sailmaker's store
53 chain room
54 trim tanks
55 inflammable paint store
56 canteen store
57 spirit store
58 shell magazine
59 cable trunk
60 store room
61 aft artillery reserve switchboard
62 air cooling installation
63 compressed air store room
64 meat store
65 pump room
66 gyro compass room
67 AA switchboard room
68 aft regulator room
69 aft DC-switchboard
70 aft central gun training unit
71 aft AA artillery plotting office
72 gyro compass room
73 AA artillery transformer room
74 auxiliary boiler room
75 store room
76 command post
77 fore artillery reserve switchboard
78 main artillery switchboard
79 fore artillery plotting office
80 fore artillery amplification room
81 radio room A
82 barbette 38cm turret B
83 barbette 38cm turret A
84 bosun's store
85 paint store
86 rope store
87 pyrotechnic magazine
88 radio store
89 carpenter's store
90 aircraft fuel tank
91 shaft tunnel
92 shafts
93 machinery store room
94 fresh water and washwater pumps
95 electrical store
96 cooling machinery room
97 oil fuel pumps
98 power plant 2
99 power plant 1
100 switchboard for power plant 2 and reserve switchboard
101 switchboard for power plant 1
102 aft AA-switchboard
103 auxiliary condenser room
104 damage control switchboard
105 power plant 4
106 power plant 3
107 switchboard for power plant 4
108 switchboard for power plant 3
109 fore DC switchboard
110 fore central gun training unit
111 fore distortion measuring installation
112 fore gyro compass room
113 regulator room
114 ballast pump room
115 cool room
116 speedometer
117 bread store

118 bosun's store
119 clothing store
120 admin store room
121 trim tanks and reserve washing water

PLAN 04

1 meteorological office
2 phototelegraphy station
3 shelter
4 charthouse
5 communications centre
6 admiral's bridge cabin
7 WC
8 cabin for 1 SNCO
9 cabin for 2 SNCOs
10 cabin for 2 SNCOs
11 cabin for 2 SNCOs
12 cabin for medical SNCO
13 darkroom
14 SNCO's WC
15 officer's WC
16 cabin for military judge
17 cabin for chief technical artillery officer (I.ATO)
18 cabin for technical artillery officer (II.ATO)
19 cabins for 2 officers
20 cabin for chief navigation officer (I.NO)
21 cabin for signals officer
22 cabin for surgeon
23 cabin for 2 officers
24 sound location device
25 ventilation transforming room
26 VHF-room
27 cabin for 2 officers
28 cabin for watch officers
29 switchboard room
30 shelter for loading hands
31 officer's showers
32 officer's bathroom
33 ventilation room
34 physical training room
35 store room
36 room for 10.5m base rangefinder
37 artillery office
38 cabin for chief artillery officer (I.AO)
39 cabin for artillery officer (II.AO)
40 cabin for further artillery officers
41 cabin for ship's surgeon
42 cabin for additional surgeon (wartime only)
43 bridge
44 bridge shelter
45 charthouse
46 shelter
47 bridge cabin
48 cabin for 2 officers
49 cabin for 2 lieutenants
50 cabin for 2 lieutenants
51 cabin for 2 lieutenants
52 cabin for 2 lieutenants
53 cabin for 2 lieutenants
54 cabin for 2 lieutenants
55 cabin for 2 officers
56 cabin for 2 officers
57 cabin for 2 officers
58 cabin for 2 officers
59 cabin for 1 artillery officer (wartime only)

PLAN 05

1 cabin for 2 artillery SNCOs
2 cabin for fire control SNCO and reserve AA fire control SNCO
3 cabin for 1 SNCO
4 cabin for 2 artillery SNCOs
5 clothing store, reserve
6 trim tank
7 chief admin officer
8 cabin for electrical engineer NCO
9 cabin for chief admin SNCO
10 cabin for chief engineer SNCO
11 SNCO's mess
12 rudder gear room
13 inner propeller
14 rudder, port
15 rudder, starboard
16 propeller protector, port
17 propeller protector, starboard
18 cabin for 2 signals SNCO's
19 cabin for chief signal SNCO
20 pantry SNCO's mess
21 ventilation room
22 chief supply SNCO's office
23 rudder gear room
24 empty room
25 propeller, port
26 propeller, starboard
27 bollard
28 aft capstans, port and starboard
29 bathrooms and showers
30 cabin for 2 SNCO's
31 cabin for 2 bandleaders
32 cabin for 2 engineer SNCOs
33 rudder compartment, port and starboard
34 trim tank
35 shaft bracket, port
36 shaft bracket, starboard
37 cabin for 2 SNCOs
38 cabin for 1 SNCO
39 admin office
40 cabin for 3 SNCOs
41 admiral's store room
42 officer's store room
43 manual steering room, port
44 manual steering room, starboard
45 spirit store
46 store for inflammable paints
47 canteen store
48 shaft tunnel, inner shaft
49 trim tank
50 shaft brackets, port and starboard
51 technical NCO's deck
52 sleeping room technical NCOs
53 seamen's deck
54 sickbay
55 powder magazine
56 shell magazine
57 cable trunk
58 shaft tunnel, port shaft
59 shaft tunnel, starboard shaft
60 shaft tunnel, inner shaft
61 trim tank
62 trim tank
63 oil fuel tank
64 38cm turret
65 trim tank/reserve washing water
66 ammunition transfer room
67 powder magazine
68 technical seamen's deck
69 seamen's deck
70 technical NCO's washplace
71 seamen's reading room
72 seamen's sleeping room
73 reserve dressing station
74 powder magazine
75 shell magazine
76 machinery store room
77 shaft tunnel, port shaft
78 shaft tunnel, inner shaft
79 shaft tunnel, starboard shaft
80 empty tank
81 companion hatch
82 38cm turret
83 machinery office
84 seamen's pantry
85 cooling machinery room
86 oil fuel pumps
87 washing water tank
88 aft AA director control tower
89 cabin for admin officer (II.VO)
90 cabin for engineer officer of the watch
91 seamen's heads
92 BÜ-workshop
93 control centre
94 electrical store
95 aft artillery plotting office
96 air ducts
97 reserve artillery switchboard
98 aft artillery amplification room
99 store room
100 aft artillery secondary switchboard
101 air cooling installation
102 compressed air storage
103 dry store room
104 aft gyro compass room
105 captain's store room
106 fireworker's store room
107 power plant 1
108 aft conning tower with 10.5m base rangefinder
109 walkway
110 hammock store
111 admin office
112 mechanical engineering workshop
113 inner turbine room
114 power plant 2
115 power plant
116 cartridge magazine
117 damage control switchboard
118 aft AC-switchboard
119 feed tank
120 tank for oil-polluted bilge water
121 lubrication oil tank
122 empty tank
123 cabin for fleet surgeon
124 officer's WC
125 commcen
126 officer's bathroom
127 executive officer's office
128 mineral water fountain
129 store room
130 machinery store room
131 beer store
132 aft regulator room
133 aft central gun training unit
134 overflow cell
135 evaporation room
136 pump room
137 main mast
138 ship's boats
139 15cm turrets port III and starboard III
140 ventilation room
141 wardroom
142 dishwasher
143 diesel tanks
144 trunk
145 shell and powder magazine
146 10.5cm cartridge magazine
147 aft AA artillery plotting office
148 aft AA artillery switchboard
149 walkway
150 speedometer
151 cabin for chief engineer officer (LI)
152 wardroom pantry
153 wardroom ante-room
154 conference room
155 cabin for fleet engineer office
156 turbine room port
157 turbine room starboard
158 lubrication oil tank
159 aircraft fuel
160 air reporting centre
161 machinery store room
162 radio room C
163 artillery workshop
164 bosun's workshop
165 artillery store room
166 artillery repair workshop
167 forge
168 hangar
169 welding shop
170 pumpmaster's store
171 walkway
172 crane, port
173 crane, starboard
174 2cm AA gun funnel platform, port
175 2cm AA gun funnel platform, starboard
176 AA director control tower, funnel platform, port and starboard
177 crane, port and starboard
178 officer's galley
179 ventilation room
180 boiler room port 1
181 inner boiler room 1
182 boiler room starboard 1
183 funnel
184 searchlight, funnel platform, port
185 searchlight, funnel platform, starboard
186 ensign's workroom
187 tailor's workshop
188 barber
189 pumpmaster's workshop
190 Junkers-compressor room
191 15cm turret port I
192 15cm turret starboard
193 shelter
194 charthouse
195 cabin for artillery officer (II.AO)
196 cabin for signals officer
197 ventilation room
198 hospital store room
199 seamen's bathroom and gas heating room
200 seamen's bathroom
201 store room
202 cable hoists
203 store room II E and signals equipment store room
204 electrical engineering control centre
205 auxiliary boiler room
206 power plant 4
207 power plant 3
208 cabin for chief artillery officer (I.AO)
209 cabin for ship's surgeon
210 isolation ward
211 sickbay
212 operation theatre
213 seamen's heads
214 gangway
215 fore BÜ-workshop
216 signals equipment workshop
217 rope store
218 radio room B
219 fore artillery plotting office
220 fore artillery switchboard
221 transformer room for radio equipment
222 radio room A
223 38cm turret B
224 NCO's sleeping room and admin store room
225 bread store
226 bosun's store
227 cool room
228 fresh water tank
229 oil fuel pumps
230 for gyro compass transformation room
231 air cooling installation
232 artillery amplification room
233 regulators
234 NCO's deck
235 combat dressing station
236 leakage pump room XVII.2
237 leakage pump room XVII.1
238 38-cm-turret A
239 NCO's deck
240 canteen store
241 clothing store
242 ventilation room
243 NCO's pantry
244 admin officer's store
245 capstans, port and starboard
246 capstan engine room
247 fireworker's store
248 tube trunk
249 chain room
250 signals equipment store II E
251 bollard
252 seamen's deck
253 carpenter's store
254 sailmaker's store
255 meteorological office
256 commcen
257 WC
258 cabin for 2 officers
259 cabin for artillery 2 officers
260 cabin for 2 lieutenants
261 cabin for 1 lieutenant
262 cabin for 1 SNCO
263 cabin for 2 SNCOs
264 cabin for 1 medical SNCO
265 room for ammunition hands
266 switchboard
267 room for 4 shoemakers
268 pumps
269 ensign's WC
270 overflow cells
271 boiler room 2, port
272 inner boiler room 2
273 boiler room 2, starboard
274 foretop with 10.5m base rangefinder
275 watch officer's cabin
276 darkroom
277 SNCO's WC
278 signals training room
279 potato store
280 pharmacy

PLAN 06

1 Aft conning tower with revolving hood and 10.5m base rangefinder as well as radar set FuMO 23, aerial dimensions 4m x 2m.

2 Aft AA director control tower with radar set FuMO 213 Würzburg, aerial dimensions 3m. During a refit in 1944, the mounting of the director control tower was raised by 2m.

3 Main artillery director control tower in the foretop with revolving hood for 10.5m base rangefinder and aerial of the radar set FuMO 23, aerial dimensions 4m x 2m.

4 Main artillery director control tower in the foretop, as it appeared in 1942, with additional radar control room and observation platform. In addition to its radar set FuMO 23, it carries a second aerial for the FuMO 27. The roof of the observation platform is fitted with a Timor aerial, wich is part of the radar set FuMB 4 Samos.

5 Main artillery director control tower in the foretop, as it appeared in 1944. Now all radar aerials have been replaced by a single aerial of the FuMO 27, the dimensions of the aerial being 6.6m x 3.2m. The console of the Hohentwiel aerial of the radar set FuMO 30 is attached to the mast behind the bridge tower.

6 Fore conning tower with revolving hood and attached aerial (4m x 2m) of the radar set FuMO 23.

7 In 1942, additional 2cm AA guns in quadruple mountings were mounted on 38cm turret B and the conning tower. They replaced the 2cm guns in single mountings previously mounted there.

PLAN 07

1 38cm turret C
2 transmitting station for 38cm turret C
3 shaft tunnel, port
4 shaft tunnel, starboard
4a inner shaft tunnel
5 3.7cm AA guns
6 WE-power plant 1
7 inner thrust block room
8 2cm AA guns
9 inner turbine room
10 power plant 2
11 power plant 1
12 10.5cm AA guns
13 aft conning tower with 10.5m base rangefinder
14 mainmast
15 boats
16 15cm turrets port III and starboard III
17 15cm shell and powder magazines
18 10.5cm ammunition magazines
19 53.3cm torpedo tubes port and starboard
20 turbine room, port
21 turbine room, starboard
22 38cm turret D
23 transmitting station for 38cm turret D
24 38cm shell magazines
25 38cm powder magazines

PLAN 08

1 boiler room 1, port
2 inner boiler room 1
3 boiler room 1, starboard
4 cranes, starboard and port
5 aircraft hangars, starboard and port
6 ventilation rooms
7 searchlights on funnel platform
8 derrick
9 ship's aircraft in their hangars
10 15cm powder magazines
11 15cm and 10.5cm shell magazines
12 boats
13 15cm turrets port II and starboard II
14 fore AA artillery director control towers
15 port boiler room 2
16 inner boiler room 2
17 starboard boiler room 2
18 15cm turrets port II and starboard II
19 10.5cm AA guns
20 2cm AA guns
21 3.7cm AA guns
22 auxiliary machinery room
23 power plant 4
24 power plant 3
25 15cm turrets port I and starboard I